ADULT EDUCATION IN INDIA

ADULT EDUCATION IN INDIA

Some Reflections

Dr. Mubark Singh
Senior Lecturer
Department of Education, University of Jummu
Jammu (J & K)

KANISHKA PUBLISHERS, DISTRIBUTORS
NEW DELHI 110002

KANISHKA PUBLISHERS, DISTRIBUTORS
4697/5-21A, Ansari Road, Daryaganj
New Delhi -110 002
Phones : 2327 0497, 2328 8285
Fax : 011-2328 8285
E-mail : kanishka_publishing@yahoo.co.in

Adult Education in India: Some Reflections
First Published-2004
Second Edition-2012

ISBN: 978-81-7391-624-1

PRINTED IN INDIA

Published by Madan Sachdeva for Kanishka Publishers, Distributors, 4697/5-21A, Ansari Road, Daryaganj, New Delhi-110 002, Typeset by Sunshine Graphics, Delhi, and Printed at Rajdhani Printers, Delhi.

Preface

Although India is a largest democracy in the world, mass illiteracy has become a great blemish and a deep slur on its part. Different policies, projects and missions have been put into services to remove the stigma of illiteracy from India. National Policy on Education, 1986 and POA, 1992 suggested various programmes for Adult Education. The NPE has rightly observed that whole nation must pledge itself to the eradication of illiteracy, particularly in the age group of 15–35 years. The Central and State governments, political parties, mass organizations and educational institutions must commit themselves to mass illiteracy programmes of diverse nature. National Literacy Mission (1988), based on the success story of Ernakulum district of Kerala State gave momentum to programmes of adult education. Total literacy campaigns under NLM are doing commendable work to eradicate illiteracy. Census of 2001 reveals that literacy rate has gone up and number of illiterates are coming down. But still we have a long way to go to achieve the dream of making India totally literate.

In order to eradicate illiteracy and universalise elementary education Government of India has launched Sarva Shiksha Abhiyan. These programmes are target specific and time bound. Our past experience indicates that we lack in planning and implementation of innovative ideas. Innovative ideas and programmes have not been translated into action as desired. Programmes launched have not been properly monitored and evaluated, even if evaluated, the recommendations emanating from such evaluations have not been implemented properly. This book is based on evaluation of adult education programme.

At the outset, in first chapter, attempt has been made to deal with conceptual and historical background, agencies involved in the programme, status of adult education and world experiences. Second chapter deals with related studies. The chapter third, fourth and fifth pertains to design, methodology, analysis and inferences.

As such, it is expected that the presentation of the material in this book would be useful to students, researchers, planners, writers, teachers, policy-makers and administrators in adult education.

Author

Contents

List of Tables

1

Adult Education

Introduction

Illiteracy and poverty are the root causes of all global problems stagnating the development of the country and individuals of the society. On one hand, illiteracy leads to ignorance and exploitation making vast masses poorer and poorer and on the other hand, poverty keeps them under constant stress in economic, social and cultural aspects. The nexus between poverty and illiteracy has been recognized. UNESCO statistics reveal that there are 885 million illiterates and an equal number of poor in the world.[1] In India, there are 296.2 million people according to 2001 census, whereas about 261 million people are below poverty line.[2]

India has passed through a long period of about 200 years of colonial rule. During this period formal system of education was uprooted and acquired a colonial character serving imperialism. After 56 years of independence, many changes have been brought about in formal education system. However, it is well-known that the existing system of education is largely unrelated to the life and there is wide gulf between its content purpose and concerns of national development.[3] Phillips H. Coombs in his book mentions the five factors responsible towards crisis in education—the rising costs, unsuitability of the outputs, acute resource scarcity, students' flood and the inertia and inefficiency of formal educational system.[4] Phillips H. Coombs data quite clearly established the limits of growth of formal education in developing countries.[5] These factors lead to the concept of non-formal education.

Concept of Non-Formal Education

Today universalization of education is an emerging concept to realize 'democracy' and 'equality'. The Indian Education Commission (1964-66) stated the nature of the transformation needed in our educational system; what we wish to emphasize is its urgency.[6] Thus, there is imperative need to explore the methods of improving literacy rate through systems other than formal.[7] In these efforts, the concepts and practice of Non-Formal, Adult and Continuing Education have emerged. Now, the concept of 'education' is not restricted to formal education and to a minority section but has been extended to Non-Formal, Distance Education, Adult and Continuing Education and it is education for all.

Singh, R.P. states that NFE (Non-Formal Education) should be treated as an alternative and not as supplementary or complementary to formal system.[8] C.L. Kundu refers that Adult Education is not an alternative; it is a necessity.[9] Education—formal, non-formal and informal—are conceived today not as alternative one for the other but as complementary activities of a single system. In recent years, adult education is treated as a part of total education structure of a country.

Concept of Adult Education

There is a considerable diversity in the use of term 'adult education'. It is used in a comprehensive manner and with restricted meaning, such as providing basic education for adults.

Adult education has been defined in various ways. Edward Hutchinson Founder-Director of National Institute of Adult Education (England and Wales) defines, "Adult education is

...responsibly organised opportunities.... To enable men and women to enlarge and interpret their living experience."[10]

Cyril O. Houle defines, "Adult education is the process by which men and women (alone in groups, or in institutional settings) seek to improve themselves or their society by increasing their skill, knowledge and sensitiveness; or it is any process by which individuals, groups or institutions try to help men and women improve in these ways." According to UNESCO Directory of Adult Education, "Adult Education is taken to mean courses of study and other activities which are undertaken by mature people (i.e., people over the age of 18) without direct regard to their vocational value. There has been a growing criticism about the distinction between vocational and non-vocational education of adults—vocational education also influences attitudes, values and development just as the non-vocational does."[11]

According to Ansari (1984, 1987), "Adult education constitutes a package of education activities and programmes for out-of-school youth and adults outside the formal educational system. This education aims at providing reliable and adequate information, better knowledge and skills with a view to improving the 'life style' and the earning capacity of the clientele. The main objective of adult education, therefore is to enable people to become confident and self-reliant by understanding the situation in which they live and in solving the problems faced by them."[12]

The above understanding of Ansari (1984) suggests that it is not a formal education. It should make the illiterate youth and adults functional and make them understand or aware of their life situation and the way to improve it.

According to UNESCO (1976:2) "the term adult education denotes the entire body of organized educational processes, whatever content, level and method, whether formal or otherwise, whether they prolong or replace initial education in schools, colleges and universities as well as in apprenticeship, whereby persons regarded as adults by the society to which they belong develop their abilities, enrich their knowledge, improve their technical or professional qualifications and bring about the change in their attitude or behaviour in the two-fold perspective of full personal development and participation in balanced and independent social, economic and cultural development."[13]

This concept of UNESCO includes formal education and ongoing or continuing education of already educated people. However, educated people will not be dealt within this text. The understanding of adult education by UNESCO is applicable in general. At the same time above concept clearly states that adult education should aim at socio-economic and cultural transformation.

According to Raghavulu and Narayana (1989), "adult education in India is one of the means of an individual's personal growth. However, through its components namely literacy, functionality and social awareness, adult education is supposed to help the poor in their development."[14]

Professor Malcolms Adiseshaiah states that non-formal education is wide ranging because it comprehends all learning outside the formal system and has no parameters of time and space.[15] The non-formal process of education itself provides a conceptual base for looking at a life-long education of which adult education is a very significant component.[16] Adult education is a very broad term, it is based on the concept of "education as a continuous life-long process" which is ascertained by International Education Commission, in its report entitled 'Learning to be' in 1972, established by UNESCO.[17] The First International Conference on Adult Education held in Denmark in 1949, stated that Adult Education has the task of satisfying the needs and aspirations of adults in all their diversity.[18]

The full text of UNESCO draft has a section on the aims of adult education and includes the following:

> "Developing a critical understanding of major contemporary problems and social changes...
>
> Developing the aptitude for gaining...new knowledge, qualifications, attitudes or forms of behaviour...
>
> Ensuring the individual's conscious and effective incorporation into the world of work...
>
> Promoting increased awareness of the relationship between people of their physical and cultural environment...
>
> Creating an understanding of and respect for the diversity of customs and cultures ...

To these may be added some aims, which tend to be more functional in their elaboration.

(*i*) to provide functional literacy education for adults who have never had the advantage of any formal education;

(*ii*) to provide functional remedial education for those young people who prematurely dropped out of the formal school system;

(*iii*) to provide further education for different categories of completers of the formal education system in order to improve their basic knowledge and skills;

(*iv*) to provide in-service, on the job, vocational and professional training for different categories of workers and professionals in order to improve their skills; and

(*v*) to give the adult citizen of the country the necessary aesthetic, cultural and civic education for public enlightenment.

Components of Adult Education

In all the schemes ever since launched in propagating and

mobilizing the concept of adult education programmes, major components found in common are Literacy, Awareness and Functional Development. These components were to be blended in an integrated approach to the programme. They were not exclusive to one another.

Literacy

The programme laid emphasis on literacy because literacy is a basic tool; of course, such literacy should be relevant to the learner's life. Learners should be able to read newspapers, instructions, signboard, and information relating to their work and activities of their daily life. It involves developing skills in reading, writing and numeracy. It is integrated with general education, which includes knowledge of basic features of Constitution of India, promotion of national integration and a deepening of cultural background. The participants are encouraged to learn about health and family planning, importance of environment, relevance of science and scientific temper for shaping the future.

Awareness

It is significant element of the programme. It aims at making the learners capable to shape their own future through inter-link of learning, reflection and concrete action. It includes sensitivity to the impediments to development and laws and government policies and the need for the poor to organise themselves in pursuit of legitimate interests and for group action.

Functional Development

It aimed at relating one's learning experience to the activities engaged in, so that one's work can be better managed. It implies that the learners would be in a position to upgrade their professional skills in the field in which they are interested to work. Acquisition of technical skills will improve the economic status of the adult learners.

Status of Adult Education in India

In order to know the status of adult education in India, there is a need to look into the background of adult education. Adult education in India has its own background. The efforts made during the colonial rule in the name of adult education were confined to certain pockets of the country and broadly linked with freedom movement. The early efforts were in the form of night schools and jail schools with account on adult literacy. Under the leadership of Mahatma Gandhi, the freedom struggle took the shape of mass movement. The aim of the literacy classes and night schools in urban and rural areas was that the common person must acquire literacy skills so that he may take part in the process of self-government. Adult education programmes were also started by the princely states of Mysore and Baroda. The outstanding features of the Mysore programme were regular classes on a massive scale, establishment of a public library system and dissemination of scientific knowledge among neo-literates by publication of a magazine, 'Vigyan'. Similarly, the adult education programme of the Baroda State emphasized setting up of libraries and reading rooms and encouraging people to take advantage of them.

Under the Government of India Act, 1935 adult education was considered as a definite responsibility of the Government. The establishment of mass literacy committees in Bihar from state level down to village was a significant development. The efforts made in other provinces like Punjab, Bombay was also remarkable. Adult Education Committee appointed by Central Advisory Board of Education in 1938 emphasized the training of literacy teachers, and also dealt with other aspects like motivation of adults, use of audio-visual media, programmes of retention of literacy and continuing education.

The post-mass literacy movement period (1939-48) witnessed a number of significant experiments in adult education conducted by various organizations such as, *Idara-e-Talim-O-Taraqi*, Delhi, Bengal Social Service League, Calcutta, Bombay Literacy Committee and Mysore City Literacy Council etc. These experiments brought home the fact that the scope of adult education centres should not merely be confined to literacy education. These centres should also be able to cater to the broader educational needs of the literates, neo-literates and illiterate adults of the community.

Voluntary efforts in adult education were taking shape in pre-independence period. The establishment of Indian Adult Education Association in 1939 as an apex body of voluntary organization was a significant event in the growth and development of adult education movement in the country.

Elimination of illiteracy has been one of the major concerns of our Government since Independence. An ambitious programme of social education was launched in the first Five-Year Plan. This Plan was integrated with the community development programme in the second Five-Year Plan. Although provision of funds in the second, third and fourth Plans was meagre, several programmes at the state level as well as national level were launched. The *Gram Shikshan Mohim* at the State level in Maharashtra and the Farmers' Training Programme at national level started during the fourth Plan were continued during the fifth Plan. Further, Government launched this programme on a massive scale in 1978 known as National Adult Education Programme. This programme was relevant to the environment and learners' needs, flexible with regard to duration, time, location, institutional arrangements and open to diversity in curriculum, teaching/learning materials and methods. The philosophy of the programme was based on the following assumptions:

1. that illiteracy is a serious impediment to an individual's growth and to country's socio-economic progress;
2. that education is not co-terminous with schooling but takes place in most work and life situations;
3. that learning, working and living are inseparable and each acquires a meaning when correlated with others;
4. that the means by which people are involved in the process of development are at least as important as the ends; and
5. that illiterate and the poor can rise to their own liberation through literacy, dialogue and action.

National Literacy Mission (1988)

The National Literacy Mission was launched on 5th May, 1988 by the then Prime Minister Late Rajiv Gandhi to equip all citizens of the country with basic skills of literacy. Mr. Gandhi, while emphasizing on the development of people said, "Development is not just about factories, dams and roads. Development is basically about the people. The goal is the people's material, cultural and spiritual fulfillment. The human factor, the human context, is of supreme value. We must pay much greater attention to these questions in future." Literacy is an indispensable component of human resource development. It is an essential tool for communication and learning, for acquiring and sharing of knowledge and information, a pre-condition for an individual's evaluation and growth and national development.[19]

Promotion of literacy has been identified as one of the five national missions with a view to applying technology and scientific research for the benefit of deprived sections of society and areas, which are critical to the country's development. The National Literacy Mission is a societal mission which implies that there has been a political will at all levels for the achievement of mission goals, that a national consensus can be created for mobilization of social forces, and mechanisms can be created for active participation of the people through energisation of their latent potential with the ultimate objective of promoting a qualitative change in their living and working conditions.

Despite the thrust on universalization of primary education and adult education in the past and present through NAEP, NLM and *Sarva Shiksha Abhiyan* the numbers of illiterates have not come down to desired level, although the percentage of literacy has improved to large extent. Following tables indicate various facts regarding literacy scenario in India based on census reports.

Table 1: Number of Illiterates/Literates in India*

	All age groups	
	1951	*2001*
Number of Illiterates	300.0	451.1
Number of Literates	60.0	562.0
Literacy Percentage	16.67	65.38

* *Source:* Census of India Publications 2001.

Table 2: Regional Disparities in Literacy 2001*

	Highest	*Lowest*
Literacy of all persons	Kerala	Bihar
Literacy of SC's	Kerala	Bihar
Literacy of ST's	Mizoram	Andhra Pradesh
Female Literacy in Rural Areas	Kerala	Bihar

* *Source:* Census of India Publications 2001.

Table 3: Sex Disparity in Literacy 2001*

	Male	*Females*
Literacy Rate for all Areas	75.65	54.03
Literacy Rate for Urban Areas	86.42	72.99
Literacy Rate for Rural Areas	71.18	46.58

* *Source:* Census of India Publications 2001.

Several studies and experiences have shown that literacy affects human resource development in following manner:

(i) Children's participation in primary education increases dramatically;
(ii) Infant mortality rate goes down;
(iii) Much greater success in child care and immunization;
(iv) Fertility rate declines; and
(v) Women's self-confidence and self-image improves.

NLM is based on thorough analysis of the strengths and weaknesses emanating from reports of Evaluation of Adult Education Programme. Evaluation reports on various aspects of the NAEP identified the following problems:

1. the quality of training of functionaries was poor;
2. the monitoring system lacked credibility, there was considerable misreporting;
3. the learning environment in adult education centres was defunct, lighting arrangements were poor;
4. mass media did not provide appreciable support;
5. voluntary agencies did not receive cooperation from State governments and procedures for their improvement discouraged them;
6. learners' participation was irregular and there was considerable dropout and relapse into illiteracy;
7. achievement of literacy level was generally below the expectations and the delivery of components of functionality and awareness remained weak;

8. absence of post-literacy and continuing education arrangements adversely affected the programme;
9. political and administrative support of the State governments and Panchayat Raj institutions was not forthcoming in an adequate and sustained manner.

The NLM concentrated on the 15-35 age group, which is crucial for the country's development. On understanding of the significance of national and social integration, productivity, a new work ethic and family planning, depends the course of India's future. The focus of NLM was rural areas, particular women and persons belonging to Scheduled Castes and Scheduled Tribes.

National Literacy Mission aimed at achieving self-reliance in literacy and numeracy; acquiring skills to improve economic status and general well-being; imbibing the values of national integration, conservation of the environment, women's equality, observance of small family norm, etc; and mass participation in the process of development. The critical factor in the success of the NLM were identified as national commitments, motivation of learners and teachers, mass mobilization, people's involvement, techno-pedagogic inputs and, efficient management and monitoring.

Strategies to be adopted were to—

(*i*) increase motivation by creating a national upsurge for literacy by (a) securing people's participation through media, taking out *Jathas*, training of cadres of youth, (b) increasing involvement of voluntary agencies, and (c) improving on-going programmes;

(*ii*) launch mass movement for literacy by involving educational institutions, students, teachers, youths, military and paramilitary personnel, housewives, ex-servicemen, employers, trade unions etc;

(*iii*) institutionalize continuing education through establishment of *Jana Shikshan Nilayams* and better use of existing institutional facilities;

(*iv*) ensure availability of standard learning material through the Directorate of Adult Education and State and Regional Resource Centres;

(*v*) universalize the outreach by extending facilities to all parts of the country.

The NLM proposed to cover various districts phase-wise for development, transfer and application of techno-pedagogic inputs.

Jana Shikshan Nilayams

In order to retain literacy, NLM incorporated *Jana Shikshan Nilayams* (JSNs). The basic purpose of the JSN, which were established in February 1988, was to enable learners to continue their learning beyond literacy. The JSN as a permanent continuing education centre intended to be established for four to five clustered villages with a population of about 5000 persons.[20]

JSN organized such activities as evening classes for three to four hours per week, library, reading room, *charcha mandals*, short-duration training programmes, sports, recreation and cultural activities. An information window to provide details of various developmental activities and a community communication centre.

The main objectives of the *Jana Shikshan Nilayams* were:

(*i*) provision of facilities for retention, continuing education and application of functional literacy;

(*ii*) dissemination of information development programmes, widening and improving participation of traditionally deprived sections of society;

(*iii*) creation of awareness about national concerns such as national integration conservation and improvement of environment, women's equality, observance of small family norm and sharing of common problems of the community;

(*iv*) improvement of the economic condition and general well-being as improvement of productivity.

(*v*) promoting recreation and healthy living.

The JSN intended to serve the neo-literates, dropouts, pass-outs of primary schools, pass-out of NFE programmes and other members of the community.

Continuing Education Centres (CECs)

The NLM designed a scheme of continuing education for neo-literates, which was started in 1996. This scheme replaced the earlier scheme for providing continuing education through the *Jan Shikshan Nilayams* (JSNs), introduced in 1988.[21]

The main objective of the scheme is to institutionalize continuing education for neo-literates. The scheme provides for flexibility in designing and implementation of CE programmes in order to cater to the needs of the neo-literates. More specific objectives of the scheme are:

1. Provision of facilities for retention and reinforcement of literacy skills;
2. Application of functional literacy for quality of life improvement;
3. Dissemination of information of developmental programmes for participation;
4. Creation of awareness on national concerns;
5. Training in vocational skills;
6. Provision of library;
7. Organisation of cultural and other recreational activities.

In the scheme of continuing education for neo-literates, CEC will be set up for a population of 2000-2500 so that it caters to the needs of at least 500-1000 neo-literates. Each CEC will have a *Prerak* and an *Assistant Prerak*. A CEC will provide the following facilities:

1. Library
2. Reading Room
3. Learning Centre
4. Training Centre
5. Information Centre
6. Charcha Mandal
7. Development Centre
8. Cultural Centre and
9. Sports Centre.

Status of Adult Education in Jammu and Kashmir

During 1931, mass revolt against the government, a demand for extension of educational facilities was made. Mr. K.G. Saiyidain implemented a mass scale A.E. Programme. Earlier to this some stray efforts were made e.g., starting of adult education school for women in 1910 in Aftab Koul's House later shifted to *Seva Sadan*, an establishment of women welfare trust in 1927. Seven hundred sixty centres were opened on 15th October, 1938 in pursuance to the recommendations of Education Re-organisation Committee headed by Saiyidain.[22]

After independence, Jammu and Kashmir State was given a special status under Article 370 of Indian Constitution. Accordingly, a separate constitution was framed to achieve the objectives of development and progress through a special programme called 'Naya Kashmir'. Extended educational facilities to the farthest and the most backward areas of the state was a pivotal issue and given due place in J&K constitution under Articles 20, 21, 23.[23]

Jammu and Kashmir government implemented social education scheme in its own way after evaluation by a committee appointed for the purpose under the chairmanship of Mr. A.Kazemi in 1950. The scheme fell in line with the recommendations of the committee wherein it suggested:

1. Opening of AE centres to be provided with facilities;
2. Rs. 20 as honorarium to local person managing the centre;
3. Literacy, health, rural sanitation and social and economic programme of 'Naya Kashmir';
4. Establishment of Public Libraries;
5. Provision for follow-up.

In order to implement different schemes of adult education in Jammu and Kashmir, in view of its specific geographical, economic and educational conditions, Government appointed different committees such as Bhagwan Sahay Committee (1972), L.K. Jha Committee (1978) and also convened a Round Table Conference in 1975 under chairmanship of Late Sheikh Abdullah, wherein operational strategies of implementation were worked out.[24]

Jammu and Kashmir is one of the pioneering state to launch the National Adult Education Programme (NAEP) on a massive scale on 2nd October, 1978 along with many other states.[25] The programme started in all the 10 districts existing at that time with the objective of making 1.3 million adults literate out of a total population of 1.86 million in the age group of 15-35 years, by the end of sixth Five-Year Plan. Since then, a substantial number of adults (6,76,527) have been made literate in this state up to ending June 1989. By ending September 1989, 18 projects –8 in Jammu Division and 10 in Kashmir Division were functioning in the state with an enrolment of 75,658 learners receiving literacy education in 2,446 centres, besides this, 7,875 learners were learning literacy skills in 503 handicraft centres in the valley. Thus, in the valley of Kashmir 1,25,358 males and 2,47,369 females have become literate up to ending June 1989.[26]

Adult education programme has been implemented by the

State government through the University of Jammu and some voluntary organizations, like *Shramik Vidyapeeth* and *Nehru Yuvak Kendras* in Jammu Division and in Kashmir Division, the University of Kashmir is organizing adult education programme through its affiliated colleges. Besides this, State Resource Centre (in the University of Kashmir) prepares teaching-learning material, organizes training programmes for field functionaries, conducts monitoring, and evaluation of the programme in operation. In 1997, TLC was also launched in the some districts of the State.

Agencies of Adult Education

Nehru Yuvak Kendras

The involvement of non-student youth in the adult education programme has also been conceived mainly through *Nehru Yuvak Kendras* (NYKs). It was proposed to strengthen the efforts of NYKs in taking up sizeable programme of adult education within their respective areas. The State Governments/ Union Territory administrations within whose jurisdiction NYK is established have been advised again to extend help and cooperation to NYKs in developing suitable programme of training and educating the youth according to their felt needs.

Shramik Vidyapeeth

Funded by the Government of India, the programme was slated with *Shramik Vidyapeeth* in 1967 to provide integrated education to urban and industrial workers. The programme is designed (a) to ensure all round development of workers and members of their families, and (b) to raise their productive ability and at the same time enriching their personal lives. *Shramik Vidyapeeths* are the centres of continuing non-formal education for urban workers, both from the organized sections, and are helping to achieve the three objectives of adult education programme, namely literacy, awareness and functionality in a very effective way.

Voluntary Organizations (VOs)

In this category, non-official agencies engaged in a variety of activities including educational, health care, rural development and village industries works are included. The role of voluntary organizations in adult education programme has many dimensions. The voluntary agencies run adult education centres in many States and Union Territories of the country. In addition, in few states, voluntary organizations have the responsibility of the State Resource Centre for development of teaching and learning material. These resource centres provide training to the field level functionaries of the State and develop need-based curriculum for learners. The Resource Centres also bring out the papers, posters and the literature for neo-literates. Voluntary organizations also serve as a catalytic agent in bringing about significant change in the neo-literates after imparting them literacy and numeracy skills. Voluntary agencies as catalyst have a specific role in providing the necessary link between various development programmes meant for rural poor and the beneficiaries themselves.

Universities

In order to make Adult Education Programme, as mass-movement university students have been involved in a big way. In addition to running adult education centres, students have to be involved in organization of educational and cultural programmes, film shows, library services etc. for the participants of adult education centres. Institutions of higher education also have a special role to play in the organization of research and evaluation and in the production of suitable teaching-learning materials.

In addition to running adult education centres, universities have also established the State Resource Centres for adult literacy. To cite an instance, the Adult and Continuing Education Centres of the *Gujarat Vidyapeeth* is training all functionaries, particularly supervisors and project officers of adult literacy programme in the state. It trains about 500 persons every year and has produced about 80 books for neo-literates including 5 primers and teachers' handbooks etc. It has a wide network of 160 adult literacy and continuing education centres. Work done by students in this field is accredited as a part of curricular studies. The university has also concluded a benchmark survey of over 40 villages to determine the learning needs of the people. The Gandhigram Rural Institute through the aegis of its centres for adult and continuing education has similarly adopted 26 villages located in 31 blocks and Madurai district of Tamil Nadu State. Members of the Faculty of the Institute involve themselves intensively in carrying out various developmental activities in these villages to cater to the needs of adult learners. Such involvement of the university in identifying models of micro-level development and involving students in carrying educational benefits to the people are indeed worthwhile initiatives. In linking the learning process to the needs of the society and involving students as agents of social change, the universities have an important role to play in promoting change.

The complexities of the contemporaneous life situations demand that education should be continuous, characterized by a life-long exposure to the ever expanding frontiers of knowledge, increasing mastery over the natural environment and a suitable adaptation to the rapidly changing social milieu. The success of a large country like India depends primarily on the quality of men and women and their access to knowledge and understanding of skills. Adult education as conceived in the National Adult Education Programme (1978), constituted an integral part of human resource development, which is so vital for any development. India has 200 recognized universities and about 7000 colleges and crores of rupees spent on education every year. The function of the university to help the social, economic and cultural growth of the community which it serves.

The involvement of the universities was well-conceived and they are expected to establish the necessary linkage with the community offering need-based and relevant educational programmes that may ultimately facilitate self-reliance. Kothari Review Committee strongly supported the involvement of institution of higher education so as to make their teaching, research and extension programme more meaningful and challenging. These sentiments were echoed in the conference of Vice-Chancellors (1981) and later by an expert group. It is generally believed that universities are specifically well suited, structured and staffed to provide the needed professional and technical guidance required for the implementation of the programme. The university is generally endowed with rich human resources in the form of libraries, laboratories and buildings. In developing countries with all types of scarcities, the resources available with the university and whatever other resources can mobilize have to be rationally utilized to promote social good to the maximum extent possible.

The University Grants Commission has been assisting the universities and colleges by providing leadership through a standing committee of experts and drawing detailed guidelines. The universities are supposed to develop need-based curriculum and teaching-learning materials organizing training programmes for personnel at different levels, preparing evaluation tools and carrying out evaluative studies relating to follow-up measures, conducting initial surveys for identifying learners and community needs, providing assistance in preparing popular literature for masses; and carrying out applied researches. This participation is secured through students, teachers and the departments or centres of adult and continuing education or non-formal or extension education.

As proposed by the UGC, the objectives of adult and continuing education and extension programmes are as follows:

(1) To enable the universities to establish the necessary linkage with community offering need-based and relevant educational programmes;
(2) To provide opportunities to disseminating knowledge in all walks of life in different segments of population for their intellectual growth and professional and technical competence;
(3) To cater to the felt needs of all people but specially to the needs of less privileged and under-privileged sections;
(4) To enrich higher education by integrating it with continuing and adult education programme and extension work;
(5) To provide an opportunity to the faculty and the students to be exposed to field experience—problems and realities and;
(6) To enable the faculty and students to participate in extension research and action research.

A working group set up to review the existing programme in the universities to identify the difficulties and suggest remedial measures brought out many problems. Some of them are:

(a) lack of awareness of seriousness of the problem of illiteracy among university functionaries, principals, teachers and students;
(b) non-availability of funds for travel expenses, material production, exhibition, publicity etc.;
(c) lack of resource/reference material available in the colleges for updating the effectiveness of the programme through personal equipment;
(d) lack of intensive training and orientation of instructors and absence of coordination among the various agencies involved in the programme;

(e) absence of effective monitoring, evaluation, research, post-literacy and follow-up work;

(f) lack of infrastructural facilities like supporting staff, accommodation;

(g) delays in sanctioning of funds and programmes by insisting on routing all proposals through various channels; and

(h) the achievement of learners in literacy was very modest; the situation about achievements in 'functionality' and 'awareness' largely appeared still more unsatisfactory.

World Experiences—National Literacy Campaigns

In the history of National Literacy Campaigns, three countries stand out truly with most remarkable achievements. They are Cuba, Tanzania and Nicaragua.

Cuba declared a national war on illiteracy in 1961. "Death to illiteracy will be number one goal of 1961" was the call of First Congress of the Municipal Councils of Education in October 1960. It was historic, massive, unprecedented attack on illiteracy. Schools were closed during the campaign and most of the 1,05,000 full-time volunteers were recruited from adolescent students. These students worked individually or in small groups under the supervision of thousands of volunteer teachers. After eight months of intensive effort, the illiteracy rate in Cuba dropped to 3.9 per cent from 25 per cent before the campaign. Many of the student volunteers, who participated in 1961 effort, played a key role in Cuba's education. Cuba, thus becomes first country in Latin America to eliminate illiteracy.

In 1970, Tanzania mobilized its population around the theme of adult education; literacy classes sprang all over the country–in schools, churches, factories and fields; and by 1977, the illiteracy rate had been reduced from 67 per cent to 27 per cent. Development programmes and actions in Tanzania were determined by political ideology and actions.

Even more impressive and perhaps the single most impressive undertaking in the field of literacy campaigns, is that of Nicaragua in 1980 mounted with the first year of revolutionary regime, the campaign was able to reduce illiteracy rate from 50.2 per cent in the age group of 10-23 years to approximately 23 per cent in five months and to 15 per cent in nine months. This all out attack on illiteracy occurred in a country devastated by protracted civil war with many of the country's youth killed and maimed, with a national economy in ruins and a foreign debt per capita among the highest in the world. Nicaragua Great Literacy Crusade was to democratize the country and had a political commitment.

These above three experiences of Cuba, Tanzania and Nicaragua are perhaps the best experiences to take lesson and to be followed by India for any mass campaign. If illiteracy is to be eradicated, we should follow the examples of other countries, which have liquidated illiteracy, like China, Cuba, Nicaragua, Tanzania. The mass campaign to liquidate illiteracy in India can be undertaken if the teachers and students of all Arts and Science Colleges, Universities and Higher Secondary Schools are mobilized to undertake a teaching campaign for a 6 months period from January to June.

Need and Significance of the Study

Adult education plays a crucial role in releasing the energy and nurturing creativity of people enabling them to meet the diverse challenges of the present world. In technologically developing society, all people are learners throughout life. The adult is endowed with plethora of collective and individual experiences as well as abilities, must be provided with the opportunity to build on experiences, to construct himself intellectually and physically and to develop both himself and his community. The commitment of UNESCO to adult learning and leading role it has played in promotion of adult education has been in clear evidence over the last few decades. In India, after independence, various adult education programmes

(NAEP and TLC of NLM) gained momentum with shifting concepts and goals of adult education. Despite commendable work done in several areas of adult education, adult education programme has both strengths and shortcomings. There is always need to evaluate various aspects of adult education like retention among adult learners, motivation, content and methodology, training of field functionaries, financial constraints, location of AE centres, provision for follow-up, post-literacy and continuing education. The present study endeavoured to evaluate the functioning of AE programme run by universities located in the northern region. The huge amount had been earmarked for eradicating illiteracy and univeralising elementary education at the national level through various agencies. But the manner in which programmes have been implemented, they have been under severe criticism. Therefore the need for conduct of study was felt to provide feedback for various agencies implementing AE programme.

Objectives of the Study

Following were the objectives of the study:

(1) To construct—
  (a) Retention Test for adult learners.
  (b) Interview Schedules for adult learners, instructors, supervisors and organizing agency.

(2) To identify adult education centres run by the universities.

(3) To study the significance of differences in retention scores of adult learners belonging to different levels of age, economic status and caste.

(4) To study the significance of interactional differences in retention scores of adult learners among variables under study.

(5) To analyse the views of adult learners, instructors, supervisors and agency regarding the functioning of AE programme.

(6) To study the organizational network of universities as an agency for implementing AE programme.

Delimitations

The study was confined to adult education centres run by four universities (University of Jammu, Himachal Pradesh, Kurukshetra University and Jawaharlal Nehru University) of North Zone.

Operational Definitions

Retention

Retention means remaining impressions of experience or learning. Described by the psychologist Woodworth as one of the four memory process, the other being memorizing, recall and recognition. Retention varies in individuals and may be sufficient for recognition but not for recall. Retention seems to be dependent upon chemical or psychological changes in the brain. It has been defined as the amount correctly remembered. The principal methods of assessing retention are savings, recognition and recall. In the present study retention among adult learners was measured in terms of retention scores obtained on the basis of administration of retention test.

Adult Education

Adult education means education provided for adults for general, educational rather than vocational reasons. Adult education may be provided by a college/university extramural department or extension studies or other sponsoring organizations. It has much in common with education permanent, life long education and recurrent education. Adult education refers to a process of imparting knowledge to illiterate adults making it suitable to their overall development by creating awareness in them about their socio-economic, cultural and political situation. It has three components (1) literacy (2) functionality and (3) awareness.

Adult Education Centres

It refers to the centres meant for providing adult education to illiterate adults for a specific period of time (i.e. from nine months to twelve months).

Evaluation

Evaluation means value judgement on an observation, performance test, or indeed any data whether directly measured or inferred. For example, if a pupil gains a score of 32 on a test of education, this measure is evaluated by placing a meaning on it relative to standard, norm or some other situation. Thus the score may be 'above average', 'fail' or indicative of below or above average effort on the part of the individual or again that the score is good for his/her age, but 'average' for his or her particular class. For evaluation, if tests are used these are called evaluation tests or instruments. In the present study evaluation was done through retention test and interview schedules. Performance of adult learners was evaluated in terms of achievement in literacy and education. Interview schedules were used to capture the views of adult learners and field functionaries.

Literacy

Literacy means the ability to read, write and do arithmetic. It is measured through literacy test.

Functionality

Functionality refers to improvement of vocational skills for more productive use of time for a farmer, for instance, it implies information about scientific methods of farming, improved seeds, equipment and institutions which can provide inputs for improved agriculture.

Social Awareness

Social awareness is understood as the knowledge about social problems legislations and policies of the government.

REFERENCES

1. UNESCO (1995) World Education Report.
2. National Sample Survey Organisation (2002), Survey 2001–2002, New Delhi.
3. Ministry of Education (1978), Report of Education Commission, 1964-66, Government of India, Reprint, p. 5.
4. Bhola, H.S. (1986), *"Non-Formal Education in Perspective"*, Newsletter, Indian National Commission for Cooperation with UNESCO, Vol. XXI, No. 3, 1983. Cited by C.L. Kundu, Adult Education, Principles, Practice and Prospectus, Sterling Publishers Private Limited, New Delhi, p. 11.
5. *Ibid*, p. 11.
6. Ministry of Education, Report of Education Commission, *op. cit.* p. 5.
7. Hemalatha, C. (1987), *"Receptivity to Adult Education Programme and Factors Influencing the Process"*, Ph.D.Thesis, Osmania University, Hyderabad, p. 1.
8. Singh, R.P. (1987), *"Non-Formal Education: An Alternative Approach"*, Sterling Publishers Private Limited, New Delhi.
9. Kundu, C.L. (1986), *"Adult Education: Principles, Practice and Prospects"*, Sterling Publishers Private Limited, New Delhi, p. 1.
10. Huchinson, E.M. (1963), *"Introduction to Adult Education"*, National Institute of Adult Education, Leicester.
11. Houle, C.O. (1972), *"The Design of Adult Education"*, Jossey Boss, San Francisco, p. 32.
12. Ansari, N.A. (1984), *"Adult Education in India"*, S. Chand and Company Limited, New Delhi.
13. UNESCO (1976), *"Draft Recommendation on the Development of Education"*, Paris, p .2.
14. Lawrence Correa (1995), *"Adult Education for Social Development"*, Himalaya Publishing House, Bombay, p. 20.
15. Singh, R.P. *op. cit.* p .2.
16. Sharma, D.V. (1984), *"In Search of a Conceptual Framework of Adult Education Reading Material* VI", Directorate of Adult Education, Bangalore, cited by C.L. Kundu, *op. cit.* p. 16.

17. Edgar Faure, et al. (1972), *"Learning To Be"*, UNESCO Paris, cited by C.L. Kundu, *op. cit.*, p.5.
18. Khan, Ferdouse; Adult Education and Rural Development, Adult Education in Asia and the Pacific, *op. cit.*, p. 141.
19. Ministry of Human Resource Development, Department of Education, National Literacy Mission (Draft), New Delhi, 1987.
20. Ministry of Human Resource Development, Jan Shikshan Nilayam, New Delhi, 1988.
21. *Ibid.*
22. Saiyidain, K.G. (1938), *"Education Re-organization Report"*, Ranbir Govt. Press, Jammu.
23. Rasool G. and Chopra, M. (1986), *"Education in J&K"*, Jay Kay Book House, Jammu.
24. Seru, S.L. (1980), *"History and Growth of Education in J&K (1873-1979)"*, Ali Mohd & Sons, Srinagar.
25. Tantray, G.N. (1994), *"Adult Education Programmes in J&K"*, A Project Report, Srinagar.
26. *Ibid.*

2

Review of Related Literature

In this chapter, an intensive search has been made to gather information in relation to the problem of study. A good number of studies were examined which have thrown light indirectly on the selected problem. A very few studies have been carried out in direct relation to the present study in the field of education.

Ahmed (1957)[1] made a survey of the literature published for neo-literates and its evaluation on all India basis. For this literature census survey method was used. The main findings were: very few persons got specialized training in the techniques of material production. Private publishers have no clear ideas of needs, interests and difficulties of neo-literates. The printed material differed in get up topics and language used.

The evaluation of literature was used to improve its quality. It was an action research. Descriptive method was employed. The data were collected through 'test passage', 'content analysis sheet', 'inventory of topics and a questionnaire'. The main findings were although no material is physically satisfactory, illustration can be improved. Majority of books are related to epics, biography, agriculture, religion, and preferred subjects. As regards the production, most of the agencies have special staff for the purpose.

Singh (1957)[2] examined social implications of spreading mass literacy and education in India. Descriptive survey method was employed. 174 Hindi books, 60 documentary films were analyzed. The main findings of the study were: the books were sub-standard. The material was irrelevant to the needs and interests of the adults. The films also do not fulfil the aims of mass literacy.

Khan (1958)[3] studied the problems of social education regarding illiterate farmers. This study revealed that even with a programme of hundred hours of instruction, there was a danger of an adult student lapsing into illiteracy, to consolidate the gains of learning, at least a total of 125 hours, followed by self-education through a library, was needed and to which minimum of 75 hours should be added to the requirement of social education.

Naik (1963)[4] intended to give an account of reading interests and habits of readers. Method used was normative survey and the data were collected with the help of an interview schedule. The findings of the study were: the most popular reading material was books, magazines and newspapers and interests in professional literature were lacking in all age groups.

Pradeshi (1967)[5] identified the agricultural education needs of the out of school rural youth. Normative method was used, and interview schedule was used for data collection. The main findings were: the youth are hardworking, progressive and keen to adopt new methods to increase production. Their educational needs and knowledge are (a) new inputs, (b) tendencies of production, and (c) economics of production. Among various topics of farm management and farm-mechanics-insect control and maintenance of pumps and engines are more popular; most of them like self-education. Various agencies of decreasing order of likeliness are: village level workers at block level, agricultural institutions, primary/secondary school teachers.

Singh (1967)[6] identified socio-economic structure of village having literacy training. It was a case study in which five functionally literate, three dropouts, three illiterates and two self-learners were studied. The data were collected through interviews, village data schedule and case studies. Main findings were: the literacy percentage was 27.3 among adults. There was no significant difference in the motivational pattern of functional literates, self-learners and dropouts.

Kakkar (1967)[7] examined that how the Workers' Education Scheme contributed to the educational proficiency of workers. Descriptive survey was used. The main findings were: that the syllabus is general in nature and in no way useful to the workers. There are less audio-visual aids along with more interference of government over the scheme. The women's education is not encouraged. Majority of workers believe that by attending classes their consciousness develops and helps them to tackle the labour management problems more effectively.

Rashid (1967)[8] published a report on experimental adult schools for illiterates. The experiment was carried at five different places i.e., Delhi, Bombay, Coimbatore, Lucknow and Mysore. Experimental-cum-descriptive method was employed and data were collected through test constructed for the objectives. The main findings were: the highest average daily attendance is 76 per cent and lowest 63 per cent. 77 per cent of the adult students have passed the public examinations at the end of grade IV and made significant progress in skills of reading and writing from grade to grade.

Chaturvedi (1969)[9] studied the impact of social education on life and living of people in U.P. Descriptive survey method and self-prepared questionnaire followed by interview of seven selected groups of people were used for collecting data. The main findings of the study indicated that farmers were mostly using traditional method for agriculture. Generally, they have no knowledge of plant diseases and their control. Social education has greatly influenced life and living of people.

Ansari (1970)[10] in his analytical study of training programme for social education workers, found that about 60 per cent of the time of the whole programme was allotted to the theoretical work and remaining 40 per cent was devoted to practical work.

Bhandari (1970)[11] studied the factors that effect the holding power of literacy classes. Descriptive survey method was followed. Three interview schedules were used—one for the persistors, other for dropouts and third for instructors. The main findings were: persistency in the middle caste group is greater than in lower and higher caste groups. Rate of dropout is greater in the case of married adults than in case of unmarried ones, which may be due to illness, being busy in agriculture etc.

Singh (1970)[12] has worked on the problem "literacy in two Indian villages", to find out the factors which motivate adults to learn literacy skills and the use of those skills. The method used was case study. The main findings were: majority of adults attending literacy classes belonged to age group 15-50. They were motivated to become literate and were able to write at simple levels. Agricultural labourers used the skills occasionally to put their signatures, others used the skills in their daily work, reading and writing letters etc.

Johnson (1970)[13] made an attempt to assess the status of adult education in Tamil Nadu. He suggested a plan of action also. According to him, first of all, the problem of wastage and stagnation at the school stage should be effectively tackled to arrest the growth of the problem of adult illiteracy. Adult education programme did not serve this purpose very much.

Shankar (1972)[14] performed an experiment in functional literacy teaching through '*Naya Savera*' method. The objective was to find out whether the period of literacy course could be reduced. For experiment, three groups of learners—one control group (consisting of two sub-groups) and two experimental groups were taken. One of the experimental group was given a nine months course and the other six months course. The contents were the same in all courses. At the end of the experiment, on experimental subgroup, each of the nine months and six months courses was examined on the old test and the subgroup on the 'new' test. The main findings were: the difference between the mean number of words reading per minute was significant at .05 level in case of nine months control group and experimental group. Control group was doing better in 'old' test and experimental group doing better in 'new' test.

Agnihotri (1974)[15] made an attempt to evaluate the programme of adult education in Wardha district. He found no improvement in the standard of living of the people as a result of development activities. The rural people had started realizing the importance of modern farming methods. A good percentage of them understood the necessity of cleanliness. The people were mostly conservative and fate-oriented and spent their leisure time in praying to God than doing any other constructive work.

Mali (1974)[16] studied the factors affecting retention of literacy among the adult neo-literates. Two kinds of factors were studied: (a) class-room factors such as motivation of learners to join the class, methods of teaching in the class, reading materials used in the class, duration of classes and the post-literacy practice; and (b) environment factors such as occupation of adult learner, his age, locality of his residence. It was revealed that the kind of reading material used was a significant factor affecting retention of literacy.

Dixit (1975)[17] studied relationship between educational need pattern of adults belonging to urban, rural and tribal areas and their occupation, age, sex etc. Survey method was employed and data were collected through questionnaire and personal interviews. The main finding was: vocational training was more useful for urban and rural people.

Roy and Kapoor (1975)[18] worked out on the project, the retention of literacy, to find out the extent of retention of literacy. Retention test and interview were used for data collection. The main findings were: rural school learners retain literacy in the same proportion as the urban school learners. The proportion of men relapsing into illiteracy was same as that of women.

Talukdar (1975)[19] surveyed the status of adult education in the State of Assam during the post-independence period. According to him, the status of adult education in the state of Assam is far from satisfactory due to variety of reasons, the important one being organizational difficulties, dearth of teachers, lack of means of communication and transport and lack of healthy attitude on the part of the universities in relation to adult education.

Mahar (1975)[20] studied the role of Workers' Education Scheme (WES) in creating trade union consciousness. Descriptive method was employed. Questionnaire and interview schedules were used for data collection. The main findings were: that Workers' Education Scheme has speeded up the productivity, safety and duty consciousness, better industrial relations in trained workers. It motivated worker teachers to take keen interest in trade union activities.

Duari (1976)[21] constructed standardized intelligence test for measuring general ability of 7 to 16½ years of age and adult age groups. An intelligence group test was developed and age norms and grade norms were established. These tests are usable for 7 to 16½ years of age and also for literate adults, however, these tests are of no use for illiterate adults.

Gayatonde (1977)[22] made the study to find out the causes of widespread illiteracy in the country. Descriptive survey method was employed and an attitude scale and questionnaire for social education workers were used for data collection. The main findings were: most of the intellectuals understand the concept of social education. The workers prefer the aspects of citizenship, functional literacy and individual development. There is a lack of co-ordination among the agencies concerned with social education.

Panwar (1978)[23] studied the overall impact of the training of farmers' life. Quasi-experimental method was used and an interview, a knowledge test and an attitude test were used for the data collection. The main findings were: the trainee has significant gains in knowledge and change in attitude. There was no significant effect of age, caste, education, socio-economic status on gains in knowledge.

Ali (1979)[24] identified the different types of leisure time activities for the adults. The survey method was employed and data were collected through an interview schedule. The findings were: music and dance were not popular rather radio and television were very popular for recreation. However, majority takes more interest in listening to music than in educational programmes. Few people like smoking, drinking and gambling to spend their leisure time. Few like sports and reading.

Shankar (1980)[25] identified the expectancies that urban women show from continuing education. Normative survey method was employed. Interview schedule was used for data collection. The main findings were: most of the women wish to continue education and proper formal education in formal institution of learning and about 50 per cent women prefer co-educational institutions. The main hurdles in the way are household responsibilities and bringing up of children.

Mehta (1980)[26] identified the vocational training needs of rural women. The survey method was employed and the data were collected through interview schedules—one for the rural women and the other for officials, and social workers. The main findings were women were interested in learning crafts like sewing, knitting etc. There is a great need for appropriate training programmes and to educate them for widening their outlook. There should be mobile training centres and courses should be of short-duration.

Rao (1989)[27] found the relative effectiveness of four methods of teaching, reading and writing to adult illiterates. The methods were; alphabetic—in which only reading was taught first and then writing; alphabetic method—reading and writing simultaneously; sentence method—first reading for two months and then writing; and sentence method—reading and writing simultaneously. The method used was experimental. Four groups each within 30 adults were taken for each method. One group of 20 children who passed class-III were selected as control group for comparison. Three self-prepared tests (one each in reading, writing and arithmetic) were the tools used for data collection. The main findings were: alphabetic method is better than the sentence method in teaching, reading and writing. Alphabetic method No. 1 was better than Alphabetic method No. 2. There was no significant difference among four experimental groups in arithmetic.

Nair (1981)[28] prepared a training programme for non-formal education workers to bring about desirable attitudinal changes and better performance. The experimental method was employed. A personal data sheet, a rating scale, a self-evaluation schedule and an observation schedule was used to study the impact of the programme. The main finding was that the programme was successful in terms of planning, preparation and execution.

Tripathi (1981)[29] made a case study to understand the problems of post-literacy and follow-up programmes. The main findings were; libraries were not doing well. There was a lack of coordination among various agencies. The rural areas, the diffusion of printed material was less than 10 per cent of that in urban areas; 75 per cent villages were devoid of newspaper or a magazine. There were no professional cadres of adult education to look-after post-literacy activities. There was a lack of coordination among various departments e.g., education, health and agriculture etc.

Selvam (1982)[30] established the relationship between the frequency of television viewing and awareness, knowledge and use of facts in agriculture, animal husbandry, health, nutrition and family welfare. Experimental method was followed and data were collected through interview schedules. The main findings were: the frequency of television viewing was related to sex, age, marital status, caste, level of education, occupation and income. It had positive impact on awareness, knowledge and use of programme both on men and women respondents.

Benjamin (1982)[31] made a case study to find out the measures to improve the conditions of poor people. Individual/group discussion, street-meeting, street theatre, drama, puppet show, music, movie etc. were used. The main findings were: people face new challenges and realize their value in society. There was an increase in the income of daily wagers.

Seth (1982)[32] analyzed different concepts of non-formal education. Experimental method was used. The main findings were: most of the officials and villagers do not understand the purpose of non-formal education. The programmes were not according to the social needs. There was a lack of adequately trained and qualified staff.

Sivarajan (1982)[33] studied the interests of Harijans towards education, reasons for illiteracy, dropouts, and obstacles in the way of education. Survey method was employed. Questionnaire, socio-economic-status scale, checklist and interest inventory were used for collection of data. The main findings were: 97 per cent heads of the family motivate their children for education but economic instability and lack of facilities are hurdles in education.

The Council of Social Development (1982)[34] conducted researches to study the functional literacy programme of Integrated Child Development Service (ICDS) in Meghalaya and Bihar. The method employed was descriptive. The main findings were: in Meghalaya among the illiterate group 45 per cent scored zero in reading ability, 62 per cent could not write and 41 per cent could not identify numerals. On the positive side 18.5 per cent of the illiterate could read correctly, 27 per cent could write the names of common objects and only 2 per cent obtained maximum in arithmetic. The knowledge about health, hygiene and childcare was satisfactory. Most of them were aware of greater need for extra-food (meat, vegetables and milk) during pregnancy. Primary health centre was not within the reach of a majority of participants to utilize the services of health staff. The officers failed to deliver goods to 60 centres allotted to them. There was no coordination among Anganwadi workers and village participants.

In Bihar, the main findings of the study were: 40 per cent of the participants were women from the upper castes. Attendance in the FLIT classes was 64. Attainment of literacy and numeracy was poor; three-fourth were unable to identify alphabets and 90 per cent could not identify any numerals. Facilities of Anganwadi were deplorable. After one year of this study in phase-II survey was conducted to assess the change or gain in knowledge. The main findings at phase-II were not significant. The outcome was not satisfactory at all.

The Directorate of Adult Education (1983)[35] found out the extent and form of integration of population education in the adult education programme at various levels. 'Postal survey' method was employed and questionnaire was used for data collection. The main findings were that population education was very much encouraged after 1978 and included in post-literacy and follow-up programmes. In the curriculum for training of field functionaries, there is negligible material on the subject and which too was not integrated. The audio-visual aids prepared by universities were not suitable for adult education.

Shankar (1983)[36] made a comprehensive study of two adult literacy primers. One primer was used on 'phonetic' principle and other on 'syllabic' principle. A series of four graded tests were used to measure literacy attainment. The main findings of the study was that there was no significant difference between mean achievement of two groups.

Yadava (1984)[37] examined the Indian experience over the

years in using mass-media (Radio, T.V.) for adult education and found the coordination between the media organization and governmental and non-governmental organizations. Two radio projects and six television projects were taken. The main findings were: these programmes earlier started were pilot projects and later became regular. The radio was effective in agriculture broadcasts. Radio for mother-child-care programme was systematic and appropriate tool.

Singh (1988)[38] made an attempt to study workers in Haryana. The main findings of the study were:

(1) adult education and training had a positive effect on workers' productivity. There was a significant increase in workers' productivity after adult education and training;

(2) the study had also indicated an improvement in workers' method of work due to adult education and training;

(3) on the literacy test workers' score ranged from 43-65 per cent after their exposure to adult education programme. In case of numeracy, the scores of workers ranged from 47-66 per cent. There was a significant difference between pre-test and post-test awareness scores of the workers. The workers showed significant improvement in their level of awareness at post-test stage;

(4) the test was significant between mean pre-test and post-test scores of workers' attitude towards adult education. This revealed that after the adult education programme, the workers had developed positive attitude towards adult education;

(5) the worker who showed maximum increase in his productivity had high score in literacy, numeracy and awareness was more sincere and punctual;

(6) the worker who showed minimum increase in productivity was an average learner. His score in literacy, numeracy and awareness were 51, 56 and 54

respectively. The worker was already sincere and punctual, so after training programme, there was a little increase in the productivity shown by him. After adult education programme there was a positive change in the attitude of this worker. He was able to write his applications, letters etc.

Murthy (1988)[39] investigated the factors responsible for the effective implementation of the National Adult Education Programme and reported that:

(1) the learners favoured the instructors who were regular and paid individual attention;
(2) the discussion method followed by demonstration was widely accepted;
(3) though the content was satisfactory, the learners wanted to know more about culture, business, commerce, marketing, small scale and cottage industries;
(4) instructors who were matriculates were more useful in implementing the programme;
(5) instructors who had joined in order to earn their livelihood were committed to the programme;
(6) mass campaigning helped the instructors to create literacy awareness. Some of the suggestions emanated from the study to improve the programme were:

    (a) arrangement of training programme;
    (b) involvement of all officials;
    (c) utilization of mass-media;
    (d) recognition by learners of grants and financial assistance available to them from government; and
    (e) establishment of mobile libraries for neo-literates.

Gupta (1988)[40] evaluated adult literacy centres in relation to their programme objectives in the State of Himachal Pradesh and found that:

(1) the majority of people who attended the adult

education centres belonged to the age group of 15-35 years;

(2) most of them joined only to learn to write their names and sign;

(3) the reasons for dropout include lack of motivation, inadequate supervision, lack of teaching and absence of occupational training;

(4) there were no post-literacy facilities;

(5) there was no system of monitoring and evaluation.

Bhat (1990)[41] studied the growth and development of adult education programme in India. The main finding of the study were:

(1) adult education existed in India even before Indian knew the art of writing;

(2) during the British period, the Commission on Indian Education System (1882-83) recommended the right school system;

(3) various models have been existing in the field of adult education such as the family/neighbourhood model.

Das (1990)[42] examined the impact of socio-economic problems on implementation of adult education programme in Assam and found that poverty, illiteracy, ignorance and unwillingness of illiterate adults, social customs, religions fanaticism, conservatism, traditionalism and national calamities like floods play a destructive role in the expansion of adult education programme.

Manavalane (1990)[43] evaluated adult education programme implemented by Annamalai University and found that 57 per cent of adult learners had attained literacy skills through the adult education programme. 73 per cent of learners had literacy skills and 71 per cent numeracy skills. The adult learners differed in their reading and writing abilities significantly. 84 per cent of the learners were aware of the adult education programme while 16 per cent were not aware. 70 per cent of the learners had a positive attitude and 24 per cent of the learners had a negative attitude toward A.E. programme. There was no significant difference between men and women, and Scheduled Castes and Backward Classes learners in their literacy attainments.

Tantray (1990)[44] attempted to evaluate Adult Education Programme in Jammu and Kashmir State and reported that:

(1) the location of the centres did not match the needs and aspirations of the people;
(2) instructors were identified from amongst the local and respectable members of the community;
(3) they were mostly youngsters who had studied upto high school and considered the adult education programme as a means of employment rather than a social service;
(4) the men instructors were mostly farmers and females instructors were housewives;
(5) instructors were trained. The quality of training was poor;
(6) the honorarium paid was just Rs. 100 p.m.;
(7) most of the learners belonged to the age-group 15-20 years. They attended centres mainly to learn some craft;
(8) the learners dropped out because of poor facilities and personal reasons;
(9) method of teaching was that of formal schools;
(10) supervision and monitoring was very poor;
(11) the overall performance was rated as poor.

Bhagria (1992)[45] examined the impact of polyvalent education of shramik vidyapeeths on industrial workers. She found that the shramik vidyapeeths played an important role in raising the quality of life, improving the thinking process, and effected the life patterns of workers.

Chandel (1992)[46] investigated the cost effectiveness of national adult education programme with reference to seventh Five-Year Plan and found that State Adult Education Programme (SAEP) was more cost effective in comparison to rural functional literacy programme (RFLP).

REFERENCES

1. Ahmed, M. (1957), "*A Survey of Reading Material for Neo-Literates in India*", Indian Adult Education Association and the Research Training and Production Centre, Jamia Millia, Jamia Nagar, Delhi.
2. Singh, S. (1957), "*History of Adult Education During British Period*", Indian Adult Education Association, New Delhi.
3. Khan, M.Z. (1958), "*The Problems of Social (Adult) Education in Four Districts of Bombay-Karnataka*", Ph.D., Education, Karnataka University.
4. Naik, S.N., "*Reading Interest and Abilities of Adolescents and Adults*", Ph.D. Education, Karnataka University.
5. Pradeshi, J.S. (1967), "*Agricultural Education Needs of School Youth Engaged in Farming*", Department of Adult Education, New Delhi.
6. Singh, T.R. (1967), "*Literacy in Two Indian Villages*", Literacy House, Lucknow.
7. Kakkar, N.K. (1967), "*Workers Education in India*" Ph.D. Education, Agra University.
8. Rashid, A. (1967), "*Experimental Adult Schools*", R.T.P. Centre, Jamia Millia Islamia, New Delhi.
9. Chaturvedi, S.C. (1969), "*Impact of Social Education on the Life and Living of the People in Block Areas*", Ph.D. Social Work, Lucknow University.
10. Ansari, N.A. (1970), "*An Appraisal of the Training Programme for Social Education Workers in India*", Ph.D. Education, University of Delhi.
11. Bhandari, (1970), "*Factors Affecting Persistency and Drop-out of Adult Literacy Classes in Udaipur District*", Ph.D. Agriculture, Udaipur University.
12. Singh, T.R. (1970), "*Adult Literacy in Two Indian Villages*", Literacy House, Lucknow.
13. Johnson, J.P. (1970), "*A Proposal for the Establishment of a State-wide Adult Education Programme for Madras (Tamil Nadu)*", Ph.D. Education, Madras University, cited by Buch, ed., Second Survey of Research in Education, *op. cit.*, p. 544.
14. Shankar, R. (1972), "*An Experiment in Functional Literacy Teaching Through Naya Savera Method*", Literacy House, Lucknow.

15. Agnihotri, S.(1974), "*Evaluation of the Programme of Adult Education in Operation under the Pilot Plan in Wardha District*", Nagpur University.
16. Mali, M.G. (1974), "*Factors Affecting Retention of Literacy Among Adult Neo-Literates*", Ph.D. Education, Shivaji University, Kolhapur.
17. Dixit, A.A. (1975), "*Study of Educational Need Patterns of Adults in the Urban, Rural and Tribal Communities of Rajasthan*", Ph.D. Education, Rajasthan University, cited by Buch, ed., Second Survey of Research in Education (1972-78) Society for Educational Research and Development, Baroda, 1979, p. 543.
18. Roy, P. and Kapoor, J.M. (1975), "*The Retention of Literacy*", Council for Social Development, Macmillan, New Delhi.
19. Talukdar, B.K. (1975), "*Adult Education in Assam During Post-Independence Period*", Ph.D. Education, Gouhati University, cited by Buch, ed., Second Survey of Research in Education, *op. cit.*, pp. 547--48.
20. Mahar, A. (1978), "*A Critical Study of the Workers Education Scheme in India with Special Reference to Their Role in Government of India Presses*", Ph.D. Commerce, Aligarh Muslim University.
21. Duari, P. (1976), "*Evaluation of General Ability of 7 to 16½ and Adult Age Groups*", Ph.D. Psychology, Calcutta University.
22. Gayatonde, N.V., "*The Problems of Social Education in India with Special Reference to Maharashtra, Gujarat, Rajasthan, Madhya Pradesh, Mysore (Karanataka)*", Ph.D. Education, Poona University, 1977, cited by Buch Ed. Second Survey of Research in Education, *op. cit.*, pp. 543–44.
23. Panwar, J.S., "*Effect of Short Duration Agricultural Training on Farmers' Beanuing*", Ph.D., Education, Udaipur University.
24. Ali, M. (1979), "*Role of Leisure and Recreation in Urban Life*", Ph.D., Sociology, Lucknow University.
25. Shankar, S. (1980), "*A Study of the Expectancies of Urban Women From Continuing Education*", Ph.D. Education, Panjab University.
26. Mehta, P. (1980), "*Vocational Training Needs of Rural Women*", National Labour Institute, New Delhi.
27. Rao, T.V. et al (1989), "*Adult Education for Social Change*", Manohar Publications, New Delhi.
28. Nair, G.S.K. (1981), "*Preparation of a Training Programme for Non-Formal Education Workers in Kerala*", Ph.D. Education, Kerala University.
29. Tripathi, V. (1981), "*Post-Literacy Activities Conceived in the Perspective of Life-long Education in India: A Case Study*", Directorate of Adult Education and Literacy House, Lucknow.
30. Selvam, S. (1982), "*Social Impact of the Telecast Programme: Education for Life on Rural Adults in the District Chingleput (T.N.)*", Ph.D. Adult Education, Department of Adult and Continuing Education, Madras.

31. Benjamin, K.M.S. (1982), "*An Experience of Rural Intervention: A Case Study of CHDSC Rural Community Development Programme*", UNESCO.
32. Seth, M. (1982), "*Motivation in Adult Learners Participating in Functional Literacy Programme in Delhi*", Ph.D. H.Sc. Delhi University, cited by Buch ed. Third Survey of Research in Education, *op.cit.*, p. 1013.
33. Sivarajan, K. (1982), "*Facilities and Hindrances in Providing Non-Formal Education for Harijans*". Ph.D. Education, Kerala University.
34. Council for Social Development (1982), "*Study of the Functional Literacy Programme of ICDS in Meghalaya and Bihar*", Council for Social Development, New Delhi, pp. 127, 145.
35. "*Directorate of Adult Education, Integration of Population Education in Adult Education Programme in India: A Status Report*", Directorate of Adult Education, New Delhi, 1983.
36. Shankar, R. (1983), "*A Comparative Study of the Two Adult Literacy Primers*", Literacy House, Lucknow.
37. Yadava, J.S. (1984), "*Adult Education and Mass Media: Indian Experience (Study Conducted for UNESCO)*", Indian Institute of Mass Communication, New Delhi.
38. Singh, Rajinder (1988), "*Adult Education Training and Productivity*", Ph.D. Education, Kurukshetra University.
39. Murthy, Samba D. (1988), "*A Study of the Factors Responsible for the Effective Implementation of the National Adult Education Programme in Andhra Pradesh*", Ph.D. Education, Osmania University.
40. Gupta, Prem Lal (1988), "*Evaluation of Adult Literacy Centres in Relation to their Programme Objectives in the State of Himachal Pradesh*", Ph.D. Edu., Himachal Pradesh University, Shimla.
41. Bhat, Seva Suman (1990), "*A Study of Growth and Development of Adult Education Programme in India*", Ph.D. Education, Kurukshetra University.
42. Das, Manoranjan (1990), "*A Study of the Socio-Economic Problems in the Implementation of the Adult Education Programme in Assam*", Ph.D. Edu., Gauhati University.
43. Manavalane, R. (1990), "*An Evaluation of the Adult Education Programme Implemented by Annamalai University in the Keerapalayam Panchayat Union in Chidambaram Taluka*", M.Phil. Education, Annamalai University.
44. Tantray, G.N. (1990), "*Adult Education for Jammu & Kashmir: An Appraisal*", Ph.D. Edu., University of Kashmir, Srinagar.
45. Bhagria, Rita (1992), "*The Impact of the Polyvalent Education of Shramik Vidyapeeths on Industrial Workers*", Ph.D. Education, Panjab University, Chandigarh.
46. Chandel, N.P.S. (1992), "*A Cost Effectivenes Analysis of the National Adult Education Programme with Special Reference to the Seventh Five Year Plan*", Ph.D. Edu., Dayal Bagh Institute, Agra.

3

Method and Procedure

The present chapter discusses the method and procedure of the study used by the investigator. It includes sample, tools used, preparation and administration of tools, scoring and tabulation of data.

Design

The major aim of the study was to evaluate the adult education programme taken up by the various universities of Northern Zone. Keeping this main aim in view, the study was designed so as to evaluate the adult education provided by the different universities through adult education centres. The one shot design was followed for testing the effectiveness of the programme. Adult learners in different adult education centres were exposed to the learning material in these centres through instruction for a fixed duration of time. It was assumed that their achievement before the conduct of experiment was negligible. The change in the achievement has been accredited to the effect of instruction and learning in the adult education centres.

Sample

Sampling is indispensable to the researcher since it is impracticable if not impossible to study a whole population to arrive at generalizations. Sample means a segment of population, chosen from the universe, for the purpose of applying generalizations of the study on the universe. Research is invariably conducted by means of a sample drawn from the population through some sampling technique, on the basis of which generalizations are arrived at and made applicable to the target population. The population of the present investigation comprised adult learners, instructors and project officers involved in adult education programme of different universities of the Northern Zone. Cluster random sampling technique was used to select the sample.

Sample selected in the present study consisted of adult learners learning in adult education centres selected randomly along with their instructors, supervisors and project officers of universities of the Northern Zone i.e. University of Jammu, Kurukshetra University, Himachal Pradesh University and Jawaharlal Nehru University. The number of adult learners selected from different adult education centres is shown in Table 3.1.

Tools Used

Following tools were used in order to achieve the objectives of the study:

1. Retention Test (for Adult Learners);
2. Interview Schedule (for Adult Learners);
3. Interview Schedule (for Instructors);
4. Interview Schedule (for Supervisors);
5. Interview Schedule (for Agency).

Preparation of Tools

Retention Test

Retention test was constructed by the investigator for evaluating adult education programme run by four universities of Northern Zone. Retention test consisted of questions regarding three integral areas of adult education viz. literacy and numeracy, social awareness and functional development. Questions, which were found to be very difficult and very easy, were weeded out from the test. There were 144 questions in the final draft of the test.

Table 3.1: Showing the List of Selected Adult Education Centres from Different Universities

Sl No.	*Name of the AE Centre*	*University*	*No. of Adult Learners*	
			Male	*Female*
1.	Domana	Jammu	–	10
2.	Purkhoo	-do-	–	10
3.	Mohalla Sarore	-do-	–	10
4.	Jandial	-do-	–	10
5.	Garhi	-do-	–	10
6.	Mohalla Barwala	-do-	–	10
7.	Ghaggar	H.P.	–	10
8.	Derra	-do-	–	10
9.	Rehad	-do-	2	08
10.	Jakholi	-do-	–	10
11.	Dangri	-do-	–	10
12.	Manjiyat	-do-	–	10
13.	Kusumpur Hill No.1	JNU	–	10
14.	Kusumpur Hill No.2	-do-	–	10
15.	Kusumpur Hill No.4	-do-	–	10
16.	Kusumpur Hill No.6	-do-	–	10
17.	Kusumpur Hill No.7	-do-	–	10
18.	Kusumpur Hill No.8	-do-	–	10
19.	Jyotisar No.6	Kurukshetra	–	10
20.	Jyotisar No.8	-do-	–	10
21.	Raogarh No.4	-do-	–	10
22.	Raogarh No.5	-do-	–	10
23.	Narkatari No.9	-do-	–	10
24.	Narkatari No.10	-do-	–	10
		Total:	2	238 = 240

Interview Schedules

Interview schedules were prepared by the investigator for adult learners, instructors, supervisors and Project Officers / Assistant Directors of the Universities which comprised sample in the present study. Questions were devised to explore certain background information for adult learners, instructors, supervisors and organizing agency. If facilitated to get feedback relating to role, played by the learners and instructors, supervisors and agency in facing various problems.

Scoring

Scoring Retention Test was done on three dimensions of literacy and numeracy, social awareness and functionality. One mark was assigned to every correct response on all the three dimensions of the Retention Test. In literacy and numeracy a learner could secure the maximum score of 96, and in social awareness and functionality 48. For Interview Schedules, the responses were counted for computing percentages.

Tabulation of Data

The scores of tests were classified in accordance with the objectives of study. For Retention Test adult learners were categorized as high economic status group and low economic status group; high age group and low age group, Scheduled Caste and Non-Scheduled Caste groups given in Table 3.2, 3.3 and 3.4.

Table 3.2: Number of Adult Learners in High Age and Low Age Groups (240 Adult Learners in Total Sample)

High Age	*Low Age*	*Total*
104	136	240

Table 3.3: Number of Adult Learners in High Economic Status Group and Low Economic Status Group

High Economic Status Group	*Low Economic Status Group*	*Total*
137	103	240

Table 3.4: Number of Adult Learners of Scheduled Caste and Non-Scheduled Caste Groups

Scheduled Caste	*Non-Scheduled Caste*	*Total*
121	119	240

4

Analysis and Discussion of Results

Analysis of data means studying the tabulated material in order to determine inherent facts or meanings. Raw scores do not reveal anything in them. These are quantitative expressions of physical and psychological observation and proper inferences are possible only after the data are analyzed carefully. In other words, analysis of data leads to judgement about the whole population to which the sample in hand is presumed be related. Analysis of data involves breaking down of existing complex factors into simpler parts and putting the parts together in new arrangements to discover new factors and relationships for the purpose of interpretation.

In this chapter, whole work of analysis was divided into different headings in order to attain desired objectives. The adult learners from the four universities of Northern Zone were categorized into three groups i.e. economic status group (low and high), age group (high and low) and caste group (scheduled and non-scheduled) and their effect on retention was studied.

Statistical Techniques Employed

In order to analyse the data collected, two statistical techniques i.e., Analysis of Variance (ANOVA) and percentages were employed. In the first part ANOVA was employed to analyze the obtained scores on retention test and in the second part, to analyze the views of adult learners, instructors, supervisors and agency, percentages were used.

Analysis of Variance

R.A. Fisher (1923 and 1935) introduced the Analysis of Variance (ANOVA). It is based on the individual differences and presents a global picture of the effect of different treatments on the criterion score. ANOVA is based on mathematical theorems previously proved and in particular the tests of significance based on problems of distribution. The analysis of variance has proved to be not only convenient method but also a powerful method of research for research worker, which has been and is being used in planning, design and analysis of research in variety of disciplines. Analysis of variance is an effective way to determine whether the means of more than two samples are too different to attribute to sampling error. The F-test enables to determine whether sample means differ from one another (between group variance) to a greater extent than the test scores differ from their own sample means (within group variance) using the ratio.

After testing the data for all assumptions of analysis of variance, the investigator proceeded further with 2x2x2 factorial design of ANOVA, to test the significance of difference in the mean retention scores (dependent variable) in relation to age (high and low age), economic status (high and low economic status) and caste as independent variables.

Computation of Analysis of Variance

Analysis of Variance was employed to study the global picture of the differences in retention of adult learners in relation to age, income and caste, also to study their interaction.

In the present study, there were two levels of each variable age, income and caste i.e. High Age (A_1) (more than 25 years) and Low Age (A_2) (less than 25 years), and High Income (B_1) (more than income of Rs. 250 per month) and Low Income (B_2) (less than Rs. 250 per month), and Scheduled Caste (C_1) and Non-Scheduled Caste (C_2).

Discussion of Results

The retention scores of adult learners belonging to Jammu University were put to statistical analysis through 2x2x2 factorial design of analysis of variance.

Table 4.1: Mean Values on Retention Test of Adult Learners

A_1	62.95	B_1	100.65	C_1	78.45
A_2	96.35	B_2	58.65	C_2	80.85

Table 4.2: Summary of 2x2x2 Factorial Design with F Ratios (J.U.)

Source of Variation	*SS*	*Df*	*MS*	*F*	*Significance*
Age (A)	17640.0	1	17640.0	17.87	Sig. at .01 level
Economic Status (B)	11156.6	1	11155.6	11.30	Sig. at .01 level
Caste (C)	57.6	1	57.6	0.06	Not sig.
Age × Economic Status (A × B)	62.5	1	62.6	0.06	Not sig.
Age × Caste (B × C)	688.9	1	688.9	0.70	Not sig.
Economic Status × Caste (AxC)	1.6	1	1.6	0.01	Not sig.
Within sets	31580.5	32	986.6		Not sig.
Total	62375.1	39			

The perusal of Table 4.2 reveals that calculated F ratio for the main effects of age (low age i.e. less than 25 years and high age i.e. more than 25 years) came out to be 17.87, which is significant at .01 level. It could be interpreted that mean retention scores of high (more than 25 years) and low (less than 25 years) age groups averaged over the levels of high income (more than Rs. 250 per month) and low income group (less than Rs. 250 per month) and caste (Scheduled Caste and Non-Scheduled Caste) differed significantly in learning.

On comparing the mean values of high age and low age groups given in Table 4.1, it can be said that low age group, having mean value of 96.35 was more interested in learning than high age group who had mean value of 62.95 in retention score. The learners belonging to low age group had more power of retention in learning in comparison to learners of high age group.

Table 4.2 indicated that calculated F-ratio for the main effects of economic status (high and low) was found to be 11.30. The required significant F ratio against df 1/32 was 7.5 at .01 level. The calculated F-ratio exceeded the required table value and hence, was statistically significant. It can be interpreted that mean retention score of high and low economic group averaged over the levels of age (low and high) and caste (Scheduled Caste and others) differed significantly in retention of adult learners.

On comparing mean values of high and low economic status groups given in Table 4.1, it can be said that high economic status group having mean value of 100.65 was more interested in learning than low economic status group who had the mean value of 58.65 in retention.

Table 4.2 revealed that obtained F ratio for the main effect i.e., Caste (Scheduled Caste and Non-Scheduled Caste) was found to be 0.058. The obtained value was not statistically significant. It revealed that mean retention score of Scheduled Caste and Non–Scheduled Caste learners averaged over the levels of age and levels of economic status did not differ significantly.

On comparing mean values of Scheduled Caste and Non-Scheduled Caste learner given in Table 4.1, it can be said that Scheduled Caste having mean value of 78.45 were less interested in learning than Non-Scheduled Caste who had mean value of 80.85 in retention.

Interactions (Age × Economic Status) (Age × Caste) (Eco. Status × Caste) (Age x Eco. Status × Caste)

From Table 4.2 it is evident that first order interaction between age and economic status, age and caste and economic status and caste and second order interaction between age × economic status x caste were not statistically significant for retention scores. It could be concluded that high and low age group were independent of levels of economic status and caste factors. Similarly, economic status was independent of caste and age factors. Age, economic status and caste effects were independent of one another.

Table 4.3: Mean Values on Retention Test of Adult Learners

A_1	69.75	B_1	100.3	C_1	88.05
A_2	86.45	B_2	54.2	C_2	68.45

On comparing the mean value of high and low age groups given in Table 4.3 it can be said that the low age group, having the mean value of 86.45 was more interested than the high age group who had the mean value of 69.75 in retention.

Table 4.4 reveals that calculated F-ratio for the main effect of age (low age i.e. less than 25 years and high age i.e. more than 25 years came out to be 7.15 which was significant at .05 level. It could be interpreted that mean retention score of high and low age groups averaged over the levels of high income and low income groups (more than Rs. 250 and less than Rs. 250) and caste (Scheduled Caste and others) differed significantly in retention.

Table 4.4 indicated that calculated F-ratio for the main effect of Factor B (low and high economic status) was found to be 58.57, which was significant at .01 level. It may be interpreted that mean retention score of high and low economic status (B_1 and B_2) averaged over the levels of age (A_1 and A_2) and caste

(C_1 and C_2) differed significantly in the retention. There were 99% chances of obtaining the same value if the investigation were conducted with the similar set of sample.

Table 4.4: Summary of ANOVA in 2x2x2 Factorial Design with F Ratios (HPU)

Source of Variation	*SS*	*df*	*MS*	*F*	*Significance*
Age	2788.9	1	2788.9	7.15	Sig. at .01 level
Economic Status	22848.4	1	22848.4	58.57	Sig. at .01 level
Caste	3960.1	1	3960.1	10.15	Sig. at .01 level
Age x Economic Status	348.1	1	348.1	0.892	Not sig.
Age x Caste	144.4	1	144.4	0.37	Not sig.
Economic Status x Caste	3960.1	1	3960.1	10.15	Sig. at .01 level
Age x Eco. Status x Caste	519.4	1	519.4	1.33	Not Sig.
Within sets	12482.2	32	390.07		
Total	47051.6	39			

On comparing the mean values of low and high economic status given in Table 4.3, it can be said that high economic status group, having mean value if 102.3 was more interested in learning than the low economic status group who had mean value of 54.2 in retention.

Table 4.4 indicates that the calculated F-ratio for the main effect of Factor C (Scheduled Caste and Non-Scheduled Caste) for retention was found to be 10.15, which was statistically significant at .01 level. It can be interpreted that mean retention score of Scheduled and Non-Scheduled Caste (C_1 and C_2) averaged over the levels of high and low age groups (A_1 and A_2) and economic status (B_1 and B_2) differed significantly in retention. First order interactions between age and economic status, economic status and caste and second order interaction between age x economic status x caste were not statistically significant.

On comparing the mean values of Scheduled and Non-Scheduled Caste given in Table 4.4, it can be said that Scheduled Caste having mean value of 88.05 were more interested in learning than the Non-Scheduled Caste group who had mean value of 68.45 in retention.

From the Table 4.4 it was evident that the F-ratio for the interaction effect of Factor B (economic status) and C (Caste) was found to be 10.15, which was statistically significant. It can be concluded that the economic status of (B) was independent of Caste (C). In other words, the magnitude of difference between B_1 and B_2 was not same, within limits of random sampling, C_1 and C_2 in caste groups. For different levels of B and C in retention, it was found that the following combinations of levels of Caste and economic status contributed towards the significance viz., B_1 and B_2 and C_1 and C_2. For significant interaction of B and C and B_1 C_1 and B_2 and C_2 were found to contribute towards the significance.

Table 4.5: Mean Values on Retention Test of Adult Learners

A_1	65.55	B_1	93.7	C_1	77.05
A_2	82.9	B_2	54.6	C_2	71.4

Table 4.6: Summary of ANOVA in 2x2x2 Factorial Design with F Ratios (JNU)

Source of Variation	*SS*	*df*	*MS*	*F*	*Significance*
A (Age)	3010.23	1	3010.23	6.86	Sig. at .01 level
B (Economic Status)	15405.63	1	15405.63	35.13	Sig. at .01 level
C (Caste)	319.23	1	319.23	0.728	Not sig.
AxB	50.62	1	50.62	0.12	Not sig.
AxC	119.02	1	119.02	0.27	Not sig.
BxC	87.02	1	87.02	0.20	Not sig.
AxBxC	990.23	1	990.03	2.257	Not sig.
Within Sets	14035.2	32	438.6		
Total	34016.98	39			

Table 4.6 revealed that F-ratio for the main effect of A(age) was found to be 6.86, which was significant at .05 level. It can be interpreted that mean retention score of high and low age groups (A_1 and A_2) averaged over the levels of economic status (B_1 and B_2) and caste (C_1 and C_2) differed significantly.

On comparing the mean values of low and high age groups given in Table 4.5, it can be interpreted that learners of lower age group were more committed to learn than the learners of high age group as the mean of lower age group was 82.9 and that of higher age group was 65.55.

From the Table 4.6, it was evident that the F-ratio for the main effect of B (economic status) was found to be 35.13, which was significant at .01 level. It can be interpreted that mean retention score of high and low age groups (A_1 and A_2) averaged over the levels of economic status (B_1 and B_2) and caste (C_1 and C_2) differed significantly.

On comparing the mean values of low and high age groups given in Table 4.5 it can be interpreted that learners of lower age group were more interested to learn than the learners of high age group as the mean value of lower age group were 93.7 and that of higher age group 54.6.

From the Table 4.6 it was evident that the F-ratio for the main effects (caste) was found to be 0.73, which was not statistically significant. It can be interpreted that mean retention scores of caste (C_1 and C_2) averaged over the levels of age (A_1 and A_2) and levels of economic status (B_1 and B_2) did not differ significantly.

From the Table 4.6 it was evident that the first order interactions between A×B, B×C and A×C and second order interactions between A×B×C were not significant for retention. It can be concluded that the lower and higher age groups (A) were independent of economic status groups (B) and caste (C) factors. Similarly, economic status groups (B) were independent of the caste (C) factors. And A, B and C effects were independent of each other.

Table 4.7: Mean Values on Retention Test of Adult Learners (K.U.)

A_1	77.95	B_1	103.2	C_1	83.6
A_2	111.95	B_2	86.4	C_2	106.00

Table 4.8: Summary of ANOVA in 2x2x2 Factorial Design with F Ratios (K.U.)

Source of Variation	*SS*	*df*	*MS*	*F*	*Significance*
A (Age)	11356.9	1	11356.9	16.60	Sig. at .01 level
B (Economic Status	2822.4	1	2822.4	4.12	Not sig.
C (Caste)	5017.6	1	5017.6	7.33	Sig. at .01 level
A×B (Age × Economic Status	2.5	1	2.5	0.004	Not sig.
A×C (Age × Caste)	828.1	1	828.1	1.21	Not sig.
B×C (Economic Status × Caste)	384.4	1	384.4	0.56	Not sig.
A×B×C (Age × Eco. Stat. × Caste)	22.5	1	22.5	0.03	Not sig.
Within Sets	21896.0	32	684.25		
Total	42330.0	39			

Table 4.8 revealed that F-ratio for the main effects of A(Age) was found to be 16.6 which was significant at .01 level. It can be interpreted that mean retention score of high and low age groups (A_1 and A_2) averaged over the levels of economic status (B_1 and B_2) and Caste (C_1 and C_2) differed significantly.

On comparing the mean values of high and low age groups given in Table 4.7 it can be interpreted that learners of lower age group were more committed to learn than the learners of higher age group as the mean of low age group were 111.85 and that of high age group 77.95.

From the Table 4.8 it was evident that the F-ratio the main effects of B (economic status) came out to be 4.12, which was not statistically significant. It can be interpreted that mean of economic status groups (B), averaged over levels of Age (A) and Caste (C), did not differ significantly.

Table 4.9: Showing Percentage of Responses and Suggestions Given by Adult Learners of AECs of Various Universities

Sl. No.	*Particulars*		*Name of the Universities*		
		J.U	*H.P.U.*	*J.N.U.*	*K.U.*
(1)	(2)	(3)	(4)	(5)	(6)
1.	Female	100	90	100	100
	Male	—	—	—	—
2.	Age:				
	High	38.34	46.67	48.34	40.0
	Low	61.66	53.33	51.66	60.0
3.	Caste:				
	SC	58.33	53.33	45.00	45.0
	Others	41.67	46.67	55.00	55.0
4.	Economic Status:				
	High	56.67	55.0	61.67	65.0
	Low	43.33	45.0	39.33	35.0
5.	Location of House:				
	Besides centre	84.00	74.0	100	83.12
	Away from the centre	16.00	26.0	—	11.88
6.	Reasons for joining centre:				
	Self-interest	23.34	33.33	45.0	55.0
	By persuasion of others	76.67	66.67	55.0	45.0
7.	Reading material provided to the adult learners by AEC's	A primer, a notebook, slate, pencil and rubber by all the centres of all the universities.			
8.	Library facilities for the adult learners:				
	Yes	—	40.0	—	—
	No	100	60.0	100	100

(Contd.)

(Contd.)

(1)	(2)	(3)	(4)	(5)	(6)
9.	Ability to write independently:				
	Yes	20	15	22	23.33
	No	80	85	78	76.67
10.	Liking to learn in a group:				
	Yes	100	100	100	100
	No	—	—	—	—
11.	Letter writing ability:				
	Yes	30	20	10	40
	No	70	80	90	60
12.	Suitability of teaching method:				
	Yes	60	65	60	70
	No	40	35	40	30
13.	Post-literacy practice for Neo-literates:				
	Yes	—	—	—	—
	No	100	100	100	100
14.	Reasons for dropouts:				
	1. Involvement in agricultural and house-hold work	86	77	55.0	66.0
	2. Seasonal Migration	—	—	45.0	—
	3. Marriage of the learners	14	23	—	34.0
15.	Whether programme helpful in raising standard of living:				
	Yes	86	67	90	85.0
	No	14	33	10	15.0

(Contd.)

(*Contd.*)

(1)	(2)	(3)	(4)	(5)	(6)
16.	Whether attendance in centre had any effect on agriculture or other work:				
	Yes	45.0	55.0	60.0	55.0
	No	55.0	45.0	40.0	45.0
17.	Whether study helped in improving production of work:				
	Yes	50.0	55.0	45.0	55.0
	No	50.0	45.0	55.0	45.0
18.	Something more to be taught for improvement in the production of work:				
	Yes	100	100	100	100
	No	—	—	—	—

On comparing the mean values of high and low income groups given in Table 4.7 it can be interpreted that learners of high income group were more interested in learning than the lower income group as mean value of higher income group was 103.2 and that of lower income group 86.4.

The perusal of Table 4.8 indicated that F-ratio for the main effects of C factor (caste) was found to be 7.33, which was significant at .05 level. It can be interpreted that the mean values of Scheduled and Non-Scheduled Caste groups averaged over the levels of age and economic status differed significantly in retention.

On comparing the mean values of Scheduled and Non-Scheduled Caste groups given in Table 4.7 it can be interpreted that Non-Scheduled Caste group was more interested in as compared to Scheduled Caste group as the mean of Non-Scheduled Caste group was 106.0 and that of Scheduled Caste group 83.6.

From the Table 4.8 it was evident that the first order interaction between Age x Economic Status, Age x Caste, Economic Status x Caste and second order interaction of Age x Economic Status x Caste were not significant for retention. It can be concluded that low and high age groups (A) was independent of Economic Status (B) and factor B was independent of C factor and caste groups were independent of economic status and age factors. And finally age, economic status and caste effects were independent of one another factor.

Views of Adult Learners

This section pertains to the views of adult learners towards the various factors related to adult education programme. This discussion has been made factor-wise.

Sex

Table 4.9 indicated that in almost all the centres of the universities selected in the sample, there were female learners. Thus it was according to the provisions of adult education programme.

Age

From Table 4.9 it was apparent that the percentage of high age adult learners and low age adult learners was 33 and 67 per cent respectively in Jammu University. It was 47 and 53 per cent for high and low age adult learners respectively in the Himachal Pradesh University.

In Jawaharlal Nehru University, these adult learners of two

groups (high and low age) had 48 and 52 percentage respectively. For Kurukshetra University it was 40 and 60 for high and low age group respectively. This indicated that the low age group was more interested in learning than the high age group in all universities with small variations.

Caste

The Table 4.9 revealed that the percentage of Scheduled Caste was greater than other castes as it was 58 for Scheduled Caste and 42 for other castes in Jammu University. For Himachal Pradesh University, the percentage was 53 and 47 for Scheduled and Non-Scheduled Caste learners respectively. In Jawaharlal Nehru and Kurukshetra University, the percentage was 45 and 55 for Scheduled and Non-Scheduled Caste adult learners respectively.

This indicated that scheduled learners were interested in learning in Jammu and Himachal Pradesh Universities. In Jawaharlal Nehru and Kurukshetra Universities, Scheduled Caste learners were less than other castes; it might be due to the location of the centres. This can be concluded that Scheduled Caste learners were equally interested in learning in comparison with the people of other castes.

Economic Status

It is evident from the Table 4.9 that the percentage for high-income group adult learners was 57 and for low-income group it was 43 for Jammu University. For Himachal Pradesh University, the percentage was 55 and 45 for high and low income groups respectively. In Jawaharlal Nehru University, 62 per cent adult learners were from high-income group and 38 per cent from low-income group. For Kurukshetra University, percentage was 65 and 35 for high and low income groups respectively. Thus, the most of learners came from high-income group from both Scheduled Caste and other castes group. Hence, it might be concluded that high economic status group was more interested in literacy to grow in changing economy of the country.

Location

The Table 4.9 reflected that the percentage of adult learners residing nearer the centres was 84, 74, 100 and 88 for Jammu, Himachal Pradesh, JNU and Kurukshetra Universities respectively. Thus, it might be concluded that most of the adult learners were residing nearby the adult education centres in all the universities. To bring the desired results same practice should be practised in future.

Library Facilities

Table 4.9 revealed that library facilities provided to the adult learners were meagre. Only 40 per cent of adult learners took the benefit of JSN Library started by Himachal Pradesh University.

Duration of Programme

Duration of programme in all the universities was 12 months.

Ability to Write Independently

It was evident from the Table 4.9 that 20 per cent learners could write independently in Jammu University, 15 per cent in H.P. University, 12 per cent in JNU and 23 per cent in Kurukshetra University. Rests were not able to write independently. Thus, in order to encourage the learners for non-formal education to improve their standard of living, it was essential to make the programme more effective enabling the learners to learn more.

Reasons for Joining the Centre

The Table 4.9 indicated that the percentage of adult learners of Jammu University joining the centre due to self-interest was 23 whereas 77 per cent adult learners joined the centres on the persuasion of others. In H.P. University, the percentage was 33 and 67 for learners joining the centres due to self-interest and by persuasion of others respectively. For Jawaharlal Nehru University, the percentage was 45 and 55 for learners having self-interest and persuaded by others respectively. In Kurukshetra University, percentage of learners having self-interest was 55 and 45 for learners persuaded by others. Thus, it was evident that most of adults joined classes due to persuasion of others except Kurukshetra University, which had more percentage of learners joining the centre willingly. This process of persuasion should be continued in future also in the areas where literacy rate was very low.

Reading Material

The Table 4.9 reflected that reading material to the learners of all the universities was the same as learners were provided with a primer, a notebook, state pencil and rubber. To yield more desirable results, more reading and writing material needs to be provided to the adult learners.

Group Learning

Adult learners of all the universities wanted to learn in a group. It might be due to the fact that learning in a group developed a spirit of competition among themselves.

Letter Writing Ability

Table 4.9 revealed that the percentage of learners having developed letter-writing ability was 30, 20, 10 and 40 in case of Jammu University, H.P. University, JNU and Kurukshetra University respectively. This ability needed to be developed in all the learners so as to motivate other illiterate adults as well.

Suitability of Teaching Method

Table 4.9 revealed that percentage of learning found the methods of teaching suitable was 60, 65, 60 and 70 in case of

Jammu University, H.P. University, JNU, and Kurukshetra University respectively.

Post-Literacy Provision for Ex-Learners

The Table 4.9 indicated that there was no post-literacy provision in separate but ex-learners could attend the centre again if desired so.

Reasons for Dropouts

Table 4.9 revealed the reasons given by adult learners for dropouts. The percentage of dropouts due to involvement in agriculture and household work in Jammu University, H.P. University, JNU and Kurukshetra University was 86, 77, 55 and 66 respectively. Similarly percentage of dropouts due to marriage was 14, 23 and 34 in case of Jammu University, H.P. University and Kurukshetra University respectively. In JNU dropout percentage due to migration was 45, which was exceptional. Thus in order to control dropout rate, the centres might be opened for the hours suited to the adult learners.

Raising the Standard of Living

Table 4.9 reflected that the adult learners responded in positive and negative responses for raising standard of living. The percentage of adult learners viewing the programme as helpful in raising the standard of living in Jammu University, H.P. University, JNU and Kurukshetra University was 86, 66, 90 and 85 respectively. Thus, most of the learners were of the view that the programme might raise their standard of living.

Effect of Attendance of Adult Education Centres on the Work of Learner

Table 4.9 revealed that the percentage of learners viewing their presence in the centres affecting their work was 45, 55, 60 and

30 in Jammu University, H.P. University, JNU and Kurukshetra University respectively. Thus, it can be concluded that the percentage of adult learners viewing no effect of their presence in the centre was greater than the learners stating the effect of their presence in the centre on their work.

Usefulness of Programme in Improving the Production of their Work

Table 4.9 reflected the percentage of adult learners viewing the programme to be useful in increasing their productivity in their respective areas they were engaged or intend to engage, was 65, 62, 70, 73 for Jammu University, H.P. University, JNU and Kurukshetra University. It might be concluded that the most of the learners viewed the programme to work for increasing the production.

Requirement of More Teaching for Improvement of Work or Occupation

All adult learners opined that something more might be taught in the centres so as to improve their work or bring more awareness in their occupation.

Views of Instructors

This section pertains to the views of the instructors toward various factors related to the adult education programme. This discussion has been made factorwise.

Locality

Table 4.10 indicated that 100 per cent of the instructors in Jammu University, Himachal Pradesh University, Jawaharlal Nehru University belonged to the rural area, whereas in Kurukshetra University 72 per cent instructors were from the rural and 28 per cent were from the urban area. It may be due to the fact since centres were located in rural area so the

Table 4.10: Showing Percentage of Responses and Suggestions Given by Instructors of Various Universities

Sl. No.	Statement	Name of the Universities			
		J.U	H.P.U.	J.N.U.	K.U.
(1)	(2)	(3)	(4)	(5)	(6)
1.	Locality:				
	Rural	100	100	–	72
	Urban	–	–	100	28
2.	Sex:				
	Male	14	28	–	–
	Female	86	72	100	100
3.	Age:				
	High	38.0	47.0	48.0	40
	Low	62.0	53.0	52.0	60
4.	Caste Background:				
	SC	33	33	50	17.0
	Others	67	67	50	83.0
5.	Educational Qualification:				
	Middle	–	–	33.0	–
	Matric	83.0	83.0	67.0	100
	Graduation	–	17.0	–	–
	Post-Graduation	17.0	–	–	–
6.	Occupational Background:				
	Agriculture	17.0	17.0	–	17.0
	Tailoring & Cutting	17.0	17.0	–	17.0
	Teaching	–	–	–	–
	Household	33.0	33.0	67.0	33.0
	Student	33.0	33.0	33.0	33.0
7.	Place of Living:				
	Belonging to Village where AEC is located	83.0	67.0	100	67.0
	Don't belong to the village	17.0	33.0	–	33.0
8.	Involvement in various activities	–	–	–	–
9.	Reasons for becoming Instructor in AEC				
	For earning money	17.00	17.00	17.00	33.00
	Interest in social work	50.00	67.00	50.00	50.00
	Obliging village/ agency	17.00	16.0	16.00	17.00
	To increase the literacy of the village	16.00	–	17.00	–

(Contd.)

(Contd.)

(1)	(2)	(3)	(4)	(5)	(6)
10.	Training:				
	Duration	10 days	10 days	10 days	10 days
	Content	Literacy and social awareness	Literacy and social awareness	Literacy and social awareness	Literacy and social awareness and cutting and tailoring
	Methodology	Lecture method, use of Audio-visual aids, story telling, sentence method	Lecture method, use of Audio-visual aids, story telling	Lecture method and use of Audio-visual aids, story telling	Lecture method, use of Audio-visual aids, story telling.
11.	Suggestions to improve the training programme	Training progra-mme to be extended	Training progra-mme to be extended	Training progra-mme to be extended	Training progra-mme to be extended.
12.	Recruitment of adult learners in AECs	By discretion	By discretion	By discretion	By discretion
13.	Suggestions for future	Linking the literacy progra-mme with some useful productive work	Linking the literacy progra-mme with some useful productive work	Linking the literacy progra–mme with some useful productive work	Linking the literacy progra-mme with some useful productive work
14.	Content of teaching:				
	1. Literacy	Literacy	Literacy	Literacy	Literacy
	2. Functionality	–	–	–	Cutting & Tailoring Literacy
	3. Social Awareness	Social Awareness	Social Awareness	Social Awareness	Social Awareness

(Contd.)

(*Contd.*)

(1)	(2)	(3)	(4)	(5)	(6)
15.	Other kinds of learning experiences	Nil	Nil	Nil	Nil
16.	Views of the instructors about the programme in general	Good	Good	Good	Good
17.	Specific suggestion to run the centre	Functional component to be stressed none.			
18.	Support from supervisor and agency	Frequent visits by the supervisor and the agency at least after the gap of 15 days.	Frequent visits by the supervisor and the agency after the gap of some days.	Frequent visits by the supervisor and the agency at least after the gap of 15 days.	Frequent visits by the supervisor and the agency at least after the gap of 15 days.
19.	Reasons for dropout of learners as stated by instructors:				
	1. Marriage of learners	17.0	33.0	17.0	33.0
	2. Seasonal Migration	—	—	50.0	—
	3. Slow down of interest	17.0	17.0	—	—
	4. Family occupational demands	66.0	50.0	33.0	50.0
20.	Suggestions given by Instructor to bring drop-outs back to AE centres	1. More motivation to be provided. 2. Literacy to be linked with some productive work according to the needs of the area.			
21.	Experiences of running the centres in relation to literacy, functionality and social awareness	Irregularity in all AE centres.			
22.	Support required in the form of literature, visual pictures and other equipment	More material to be provided.			

involvement was from the rural area. Moreover, honorarium paid to instructors was so meagre that hardly anyone from the urban area preferred to work as instructor in rural AE centre.

Sex

From Table 4.10 it was evident that the percentage of female instructors was greater than that of male instructors, which was in accordance with provisions. For Jammu University, percentage of female instructors was 86 per cent and male instructors were 14 per cent only. In Himachal Pradesh University, percentage of female instructors was greater than male instructors as percentage of female instructors was 72 and that of male instructors was 28. In Kurukshetra and Jawaharlal Nehru University 100 per cent instructors were female.

Age

The Table 4.10 revealed that 38.44 per cent adult learners were in the high age group and 61.66 per cent were in the low age group in Jammu University. For Himachal Pradesh University, percentage was 46.67 and 53.33 for the high and low age groups respectively. In Jawaharlal Nehru University, 48.34 per cent were belonging to high age group and 51.66 per cent to low age group.

For the Kurukshetra University, percentage was 40 and 60 for high and low age group respectively. Thus it can be concluded that higher age group was less interested than lower age group. It might be due to the growing environment that population less than 25 years of age is feeling it difficult to live in this age of science and technology without literacy and education.

Occupational Background

Table 4.10 reflected that percentage of instructors having household/occupational background was greater than other occupations in Jammu University. The percentage of instructor involved in household occupation was found to be 33.33. The percentage of instructors involved in agriculture, and in tailoring and cutting, 16.67 per cent, whereas 33 per cent instructors were basically students. Thus, it was clear that most of instructors were engaged in household activities. It may be due to the fact that instructors were mostly female and were involved in household activities.

In Jawaharlal Nehru University, as Table 4.10 revealed percentage of instructors having household occupation was 66.67 and rest 33.33 per cent were the students.

For Himachal Pradesh University instructors involved in agriculture were 16.67 per cent, in cutting and tailoring 16.67 per cent and in household 33.33.

In Kurukshetra University, 16.67 per cent instructors were involved in agriculture, 16.67 per cent were teachers, 33.33 per cent were students and 33.33 were engaged in household activities.

Caste Background

Table 4.10 revealed that percentage of instructors belonging to Non-Scheduled Caste was greater than the instructors belonging to the Scheduled Caste. In Jammu University, percentage of instructors was 66 and 34 for Non-Scheduled and Scheduled Caste respectively. For Himachal Pradesh University, percentage of instructors was 66 and 34 for Non-Scheduled and Scheduled Caste respectively. In Jawaharlal Nehru University percentage of instructors belonging to Scheduled Caste and Non-Scheduled Caste was fifty-fifty. In Kurukshetra University the percentage of Non-Scheduled Caste instructors was 83.33 and for Scheduled Caste it was 16.67 per cent.

Educational Qualification

Table 4.10 revealed that in Jammu University percentage of instructors having Matric (10th) qualification was 83.33 and having post-graduation qualification was 16.67. For Himachal Pradesh University, percentage was 83.33 for Matriculate instructors, and 16.67 for graduate instructors. In Jawaharlal Nehru University, percentage of instructors having Middle qualification was 66.67 and 33 for Matriculates. For Kurukshetra University, percentage of instructors having Matric qualification was 100.

Place of Living of Instructors

Table 4.10 reflected that percentage of instructors of Jammu University belonged to the same locality where adult education centres were located, was 83.33. Percentage of instructors who did not belong to the same locality was 16.67. For Himachal Pradesh 66.67 per cent instructors belonged to the same locality and 33.33 per cent were outsiders. In Jawaharlal Nehru University, all the instructors belonged to the same locality. In Kurukshetra University, 66.67 per cent instructors belonged to the same locality and 33.33 did not belong to the villages in which AE centres were located.

It is evident that most of instructors were from the same locations where adult education centres were opened, as it was convenient for them to serve there.

Involvement in Various Activities

Instructors were not involved in any activity other than teaching adult learners.

Reasons for Becoming Instructors in AE Centres

Table 4.10 indicated the reasons for becoming instructor in the Adult Education Centres. A high percentage of instructors accepted the work due to zeal to do social service. In Jammu University 50 per cent of the instructors accepted the assignment, as they were interested in social work. 16.67 per cent accepted this work for monetary incentive and 16.67 per cent became instructors in order to oblige village/agency, 16.67 per cent accepted to work as instructors so as to increase the literacy of village.

In Himachal Pradesh University, 66.67 per cent instructors accepted the work as instructors as they were interested in social work. 16.67 per cent became instructors for earning money and 16.67 for obliging village/agency.

In Jawaharlal Nehru University, 50 per cent of the instructors accepted the work, as they were interested in social service. While 17 per cent became instructors, as they obliged agency/village and 17 per cent became instructors as they were interested in increasing the literacy of the village whereas 16 per cent became instructors due to economic compulsion.

In Kurukshetra University, 50 per cent of the instructors accepted the work, as they were interested in social work whereas 33 per cent accepted the work to earn money, 17 per cent became instructors on the persuasion of the agency.

Training of Instructors

Table 4.10 indicated that duration of training of instructors was 10 days in all the universities. Content included literacy and social awareness in all the universities. Methodology used was lecture method and all the universities included some audio-visual aids.

Suggestions to Improve Training Programme

Majority of instructors suggested that training period should be extended to more days.

Selection of Adult Learners

Table 4.10 revealed that in all universities adult learners were enrolled in AE centres by the instructors on their own discretions.

Problems in Identifying Adult Learners

Instructors did not face any problem in identification of adult learners as the centres were opened in only those areas where adult illiterates were optimum.

Suggestions for Future

Majority of Instructors in all the universities suggested that literacy programme should be linked with some useful productive work and skills.

Content of Teaching

Almost all the universities laid stress on acquisition of literacy viz., reading, writing and arithmetic. Some information was provided about social events. The general information about agriculture, family welfare, health and sanitation, observance of small family norm etc. was also provided by the instructors. The cutting and tailoring training was linked with literacy in Kurukshetra University, which increased the enrolment and attendance of adult learners.

Method of Teaching

The methods used by instructors of various universities were lecture method, sentence method and story-telling method.

View About the Programme in General

All the instructors of AE centres of various universities responded that the programme in general was good.

Specific Suggestions to Run the Centre

It was stated by almost all the instructors that the functional component of the adult education should be stressed more.

Table 4.11: Showing Responses/Percentage of Responses of Supervisors of Various Universities

Sl. No.	*Statement*		*Name of the Universities*			
			J.U	*H.P.U.*	*J.N.U.*	*K.U.*
(1)	(2)		(3)	(4)	(5)	(6)
1.	Age:	Low	–	–	–	–
		High	100	100	100	100
2.	Sex:	Male	100	–	–	100
		Female	–	100	100	–
3.	Educational Background:					
	1. Matric		–	100	100	–
	2. Graduate		100	–	–	–
	3. P. Graduate		–	--	–	100
4.	Caste Background:					
	1. SC		–	–	–	100
	2. Others		100	100	100	–
5.	Experience		One year	One year	–	Three Years
6.	Length of service in the agency		Three years	Two years	Two years	Three years
7.	Involvement in activities		Motivating adult learners for non-formal education	Motivating adult learners for non-formal education	Forming of Mahila Mandals	Social work.
8.	Strategies used in:					
	1.	Identification of villages (for opening AE centres)	Low literacy rate	On the recommendation of village Sarpanch	As recommended by the agency	As recommended by the agency
	2.	Location of AECs	In low literacy rate area	In low literacy rate area	In low literacy rate area	In low literacy rate Area
	3.	Identification of Instructors	Availability and interest in teaching adults	Availability and interest in teaching adults	Availability and interest in teaching adults	Availability and interest in teaching adults.

(*Contd.*)

(*Contd.*)

(1)	(2)	(3)	(4)	(5)	(6)
	4. Monitoring of AECs activities	Visiting centres and asking questions to adult learners	Visiting centres and asking questions to adult learners	Visiting centres and asking questions to adult learners	Visiting centres and asking questions to adult learners.
9.	Reasons for choosing assignment	On recommendation of B.D.O.	Interest in social work	Interest in social work	Interest in the field of adult education.
10.	Difficulties faced in relation to:				
	1. Training	Training period not appropriate.			
	2. Supply of material	Material was not adequate.			
	3. Motivation of learners	Difficult to motivate in the very first instance.			
11.	Programme as it is running	Appropriate	Appreciable but implementation was poor	Appropriate	Appropriate
12.	Suggestions to improve the programme	Functionality and general awareness should be stressed more	Monetary incentives should be given to the learners	Functional component should be stressed more	Adult pictures and cultural shows should be arranged and longer period for teaching.
13.	Evaluation of performance of instructors	By visiting centres and getting the responses of questions from adult learners.			
14.	Kinds of tools used in evaluating the performance of instructors	Only by asking questions from the adult learners.			

(*Contd.*)

(*Contd.*)

(1)	(2)	(3)	(4)	(5)	(6)
15.	Procedure for bringing improvement after evaluation	Instructors were told about the weaknesses and asked to improve accordingly.			
16.	Frequency of visits to the centres	Fort-nightly	After one month	Fort-nightly	After every week.

Views of Supervisors

This section pertains to the views of supervisors towards the various factors related to adult education programme. This discussion has been made factorwise for all the universities.

Age

Table 4.11 revealed that 100 per cent of the supervisors for all the four universit es selected in the sample were in the high age group (i.e. more than 25 years). It means that matured personnel were engaged in the task of supervising the adult education centres.

Sex

The Table 4.11 revealed that the percentage of male supervisors was 100 per cent for the Jammu and Kurukshetra University, whereas the percentage of female supervisors for Himachal Pradesh and Jawaharlal Nehru University was 100 per cent. It was mainly due to availability of the persons in the area where centres were located.

Educational Background

The Table 4.11 reflected that the percentage of supervisors having graduation qualification was 100 per cent for Jammu University. In H.P. University, Jawaharlal Nehru University, all the supervisors were matriculates. In Kurukshetra University supervisors were post-graduates.

Caste Background

Table 4.11 revealed that percentage of Non-Scheduled Caste supervisors was 100 in Jammu, Himachal Pradesh and Jawaharlal Nehru University whereas in Kurukshetra University Scheduled Castes supervisors were 100 per cent. It was also based on the availability of the persons in the area.

Experience

Almost all the supervisors were experienced except in Jawaharlal Nehru University.

Service in Agency

The Table 4.11 reflected that all the supervisors had served in the universities in adult education programme.

Involvement in Activities

The Table 4.11 reveals that supervisors of Jammu University and H.P. University were involved in motivating the adults for non-formal education. In Jawaharlal Nehru University, supervisors were involved in forming mahila mandals for the welfare of women. In Kurukshetra, supervisors were involved in social work.

Strategies Used

Villages for opening adult education centres were identified on the basis of low literacy rate. Asking learners some questions relating to the instructions when supervisors visited the centres did monitoring of AE centres.

Reasons for Choosing the Assignment

In Jammu University supervisors took the assignment on the recommendation of Block Development Officer in Himachal

Pradesh University, due to interest in social service, in Jawaharlal Nehru University, assignment was chosen due to interest in women welfare and supervisors of Kurukshetra University took the assignment due to interest in the field of adult education.

Difficulty faced in the Supply of Material

Table 4.11 revealed that material supplied by the universities was less than the required.

Motivation of the Learners

Table 4.11 depicted that it was found difficult to motivate the learners in the very first instance in all the universities.

Views About the Programme Running

Table 4.11 reflected that supervisors of Jammu University, Jawaharlal Nehru University and Kurukshetra University found that programme in general was appropriate. Supervisors of H.P. University found lack of proper implementation of the programme.

Suggestions to Improve Programme

Supervisors of Jammu University, JNU suggested that functional and social awareness component of adult education should be given more emphasis. Whereas supervisors of H.P. University suggested that monetary incentive should be given to the learners. Supervisors of Kurukshetra University suggested that films and cultural shows should be organized to make programme more interesting.

Evaluation of Instructors' Performance

Table 4.11 reflects that supervisors of all universities evaluated the performance of the instructors by visiting AE centres and asking questions to adult learners.

Procedure for Bringing Improvement After Evaluation

There was no specific procedure of making improvement in programme after evaluation except by instructing instructors verbally to remove their deficiencies and weaknesses.

Frequency of Visits to Centres

Table 4.11 indicates the varying frequency of visits to the AE centres by the supervisors. In Jammu University supervisors visited the centres twice a month, in H.P. University once a month, in J.N.U. twice a month and Kurukshetra University four times a month.

Views of Project Officers

This section pertains to the views of project officers towards the various factors related to the adult education programme.

Year of Launching the AE Programme

The Table 4.12 reveals that the programme was launched in the year 1979 in all the universities. It was after this when the programme was renamed as National Adult Education Programme (NAEP) on October 2, 1978.

Number of Centres Run by the University

The Table 4.12 indicates that the centres in all the universities were located in rural/slum areas only. There was variation in the number of AE centres under the four universities. Jammu University had 30 centres, H.P. University had 25 centres, Jawaharlal Nehru University and Kurukshetra University had 10 Adult Education centres each.

Reasons for Starting Centres

The Table 4.12 reveals that the centres in Jammu University were opened on the recommendations of Block Development

Table 4.12: Showing Responses/Percentage of Responses of Project Officers of the Various Universities

Sl. No.	*Statement*	*Name of the Universities*			
		J.U	*H.P.U.*	*J.N.U.*	*K.U.*
(1)	(2)	(3)	(4)	(5)	(6)
1.	Year of launching adult education programme	1979	1979	1979	1979
2.	Whether centres started simultaneously	Yes	Yes	Yes	Yes
3.	Number of centres run by the University				
	1. Area	Rural	Rural	Slum	Rural
	2. For male	–	–	–	–
	3. For female	20	25	10	10
	4. Mixed	10	5	–	–
4.	Reasons for starting centres	Backwardness of area/people, on the Recommendation of B.D.O.	Backwardness of area/people and initiative of people	Backwardness of the people	Area Development approach.
5.	Number of centres recommended by agency and sanctioned by UGC	All centres recommended by universities were sanctioned by UGC.			
6.	Methods of selecting supervisors and instructors	On the basis of information received and conducting interviews of the candidates.			
7.	Material provided	Primers, slates, exercise books, pencil, rubbers etc.			
8.	Follow-up activities	Instructors and functionaries visited the areas where centres were closed and distributed the reading material to out gone learners.			
9.	Continuity of the programme	All the universities continued the programme.			
10.	Change in location of centres	From one locality to another.			

(Contd.)

(*Contd.*)

(1)	(2)	(3)	(4)	(5)	(6)
11.	Change in respect of target groups	–	–	–	From male to female
12.	Time involved in submitting the proposal and receiving grants from UGC	One year	One year	One year	One year
13.	Whether grants received in time	Yes	Yes	Yes	Yes
14.	Grants adequate to meet needs	Yes	Yes	Yes	Yes
15.	Opinions regarding the programme	Satisfactory	Casual	Casual	Satisfactory
16.	Major difficulties in running centres	Part time instructors, supervisors lack of funds, inconvenient to reach the centres	Linking the programme with some productive work, appointment of staff on permanent basis	Staff appoint on permanent basis and introduction of MPFL	Introduction of MPFL and permanent staff.
17.	Significant learning experiences	Learners were more interested in learning skills for their economic upliftment.			
18.	Vocations included in functional component	Nil	Nil	Nil	Cutting and tailoring.

Officer in the backward area. In H.P. University centres were opened on the basis of backwardness and initiative of the people. In JNU, centres were opened on the basis of area predominantly inhabited by illiterate population in slum area. In Kurukshetra University, centres were opened under the scheme of Area Development Approach.

Training

(*i*) *Instructors*: Training to instructors was provided by Adult and Continuing Education Departments in the Universities.

(*ii*) *Duration*: The duration of training ranged from 7 to 10-day for 7 hours in almost all the universities.

(*iii*) *Place of Training*: The Table 4.12 depicts that training was imparted in the university campus in all the universities.

(*iv*) *Methods Used*: The Table 4.12 depicts the dominant method used in training in various universities was lecture. Lectures of experts in various fields were also organized. Film shows were also used in the training programme.

Supervisors

Training of supervisors was similar to the training of instructors.

Material Provided in the Centres

The same material was provided by all the universities, which included slate, primer, a notebook, pencil, slati and rubber.

Follow-up Activities

There were no proper follow-up activities in various universities except for one that was H.P. University where Jan Shikshan Nilayam was established for neo-literates.

Continuity of Programme

Table 4.12 reflects that all universities continued the programme of adult education since 1979.

Change in Respect of Target Groups

No change was made in respect of target groups except for Kurukshetra University where a change from male group to female group was made.

Change in Method of Selection of Staff

No change was made in method of selection of staff except H.P. University which selected instructors on the basis of interview and required the aspirants to prepare the survey and report of the villages having illiterate adult population.

Time Involved in Submitting Proposal and Receiving Grants from UGC

Time involved in submission of proposal and release/sanction of grant was one year in all the universities.

Receiving Grant in Time and Its Adequacy to Meet Needs

All the universities except in Kurukshetra University received the grant on time but these were not considered adequate as suggested by Kurukshetra University.

Opinions Regarding the Success of Centre

Centres were considered to be successful by Jammu and Kurukshetra University and casual by JNU and H.P. University.

Major Difficulties in Running Centres

Major difficulties in running AE centres were: part-time instructors and supervisors; lack of adequate funds and lack of vehicles to reach the centres etc.

Suggestions to Improve AE Programme

The suggestions of project officers to improve the programme were: to appoint staff on permanent basis; relating programme with some productive work; introduction of MPFL.

Learning Experience

Project officers were of the opinion that programme should include skills for economic development of the learners.

Vocations Included in the Programme

Table 4.12 depicts that no vocation/ functional education was provided in the AE centres except for Kurukshetra University, which introduced cutting and tailoring along with literacy for female adults.

5

Inferences and Educational Implications

Inferences

Following inferences were drawn on the basis of results:

1. Adult learners with high and low age of results differed significantly in retention. The adult learners of lower age group were better in retention than higher age group.
2. Adult learners with high and low income differed significantly in retention except Kurukshetra University. It can be concluded that adult learners of higher economic status group were more inclined towards adult education than adult learners of lower economic status group.
3. There was no significant difference in retention between Scheduled Caste and Non-Scheduled Caste adult learners.
4. There were no interactional differences in retention between age and economic status, economic status and caste, age and caste and age x economic x caste except H.P. University where interactional differences in retention between economic status and caste were found significant.
5. The conclusions based on the information obtained with the help of interview schedule for adult learners are:
   (*i*) The percentage of femalc adult learners was more than male adult learners.

(*ii*) The percentage of lower age group was higher than the higher age group.

(*iii*) The Scheduled Caste learners were having more percentage than the other castes.

(*iv*) The number of adult learners belonging to higher economic status surpassed lower economic status.

(*v*) The percentage of local adult learners was more than outsiders.

(*vi*) There were no adequate library facilities for adult learner except in H.P. University where JSN (Jan Shikshan Nilayam) was functioning.

(*vii*) Most of learners could not write independently.

(*viii*) The percentage of learners joining the centres on the persuasion of others was higher than those who joined the centres willingly.

(*ix*) All the adult learners liked to learn in groups.

(*x*) Methods of teaching were stated adequate by majority of adult learners.

(*xi*) There was no post-literacy provision in adult education programme except joining the centres again as stated by the adult learners.

(*xii*) Majority of adult learners stated reason for drop-out from AE centres as family-occupational demands.

(*xiii*) Most of the learners stated that programme could raise their standard of living and production in work.

6. The conclusions based on the information of interview scheduled administered on instructors are:

(*i*) Most of the instructors belonged to the rural areas where adult education centres were located.

(*ii*) Percentage of female instructors was more than male instructors.

(*iii*) The percentage of lower age group (less than 25 years age) was higher than high age group (more than 25 years age).

(*iv*) Most of the instructors were involved in agricultural household activities.

(*v*) Most of the instructors belonged to Non-Scheduled Caste group.

(*vi*) The percentage of matriculate instructors was higher.

(*vii*) Adult education centres were located in rural areas only.

(*viii*) A high percentage of instructors stated that they had accepted work due to zeal to do social work.

(*ix*) Duration of training ranged from 7 to 10 days for all the instructors.

(*x*) A high percentage of instructors suggested inclusion of some training for adult learners to enhance their income.

7. The conclusions reached on the basis of responses obtained on Interview Schedule for Supervisors of Adult Education Centres. Following are the conclusions reached at:

(*i*) A high percentage of supervisors belonged to higher age (more than 25 years age).

(*ii*) Male supervisors were more than female supervisors.

(*iii*) Most of the supervisors were having matric qualification. However, for Jammu and Kurukshetra Universities, the supervisors were graduate and post-graduate respectively in terms of qualification.

(*iv*) Supervisors were belonging to general category caste except in Kurukshetra University to which supervisor belonged to Scheduled Caste.

(*v*) Most of the supervisors had experience in the adult education.

(*vi*) Supervisors were involved in motivating adults for literacy, in forming mahila mandals and in social work.

(*vii*) The supervisors evaluated the performance of centres by asking questions from adult learners related to literacy.

(*viii*) There were various reasons for choosing assignment as a supervisor. The reasons were: assignment accepted on the recommendation of BDO, due to interest in social work, due to interest in women welfare and due to interest in adult education.

(*ix*) Supervisors considered material supplied by the universities less than the required.

(*x*) The supervisors found it difficult to motivate adults for adult education in the very first instance.

(*xi*) Supervisors visited the centres at the frequency of one to four times a month.

(*xii*) There was no specific criterion for evaluating the performance of instructors.

(*xiii*) Suggestions given by the supervisors regarding the adult education programme were to give emphasis on the functionality, general awareness, to extend period of training and to give some momentary incentive.

8. Conclusions drawn from the responses from project officers on interview schedule are as under—

(*i*) The adult education programme was launched in the year 1979 in all the universities included in the sample.

(*ii*) The number of adult education centres run by universities ranged from 10 to 30.

(*iii*) Reasons stated by project officers for starting adult education centres were low literacy rate in the area and area development approach.

(*iv*) The follow up activities included only distribution of reading material to neo-literates.

(*v*) Time involved in submitting proposal and receiving grants was almost one year.

(*vi*) The centres were changed from one locality to another after completion of the course.

(*vii*) Grants were received on time but were not adequate as stated by Project Officer of Kurukshetra University.

(*viii*) Major difficulties pointed out by project officers were part-time instructors and supervisors, lack of adequate funds, and lack of vehicles for timely visits to the centres.

(*ix*) Suggestions made by the project officers to improve the programme were: appointment of staff on permanent basis; relating the programme with some productive work; and introduction of MPFL.

Educational Implications

The present study has bearing for the researchers, educationists and planners in the field of adult education.

The study indicates that adult learners with high age group were lagging behind the low age group. There was need to motivate the adult learners in high age group by making them clear about importance of adult education for the development of individual in particular and society in general.

Another implication of the present study was that adult learners in low-income group retained less material. They needed to be told importance of adult education for the improvement of their economic condition.

The present study indicates that the percentage of high age group was less than low age group. High age group needed to be motivated by enriching the environment of adult education centres.

Most of the instructors serving in AECs were Non-Scheduled Caste. To make Scheduled Caste population literate, it would be desirable to appoint instructors from within Scheduled Caste where Scheduled Caste adult learners in AE centre dominated.

Another implication of the present study is that period of training of instructors and supervisors were inadequate and needed to enhance for more time.

Study indicated that adult learners were not self-motivated and there was need to create awareness among illiterate adults to join adult educational classes. They could not write independently thus required more literacy and cognitive skills to be incorporated in the curriculum for adult learners.

Another implication of the present study is that there was no provision of post-literacy education. Government of India through its programme should open more post-literacy and continuing education centres in order to reduce chances of relapsing into illiteracy.

Another implication for the administrators, the government and planners is that there was lack of provision of functional literacy in the ongoing programme of adult education. In order to attract illiterate adults towards adult education centres, functional training was to be made most important component of adult education programme as adult learners, instructors, supervisors and project officers suggested it to be emphasized more than other aspects.

Major reason for dropout found in the present study was family/occupational demands. Thus, it was implied that adult education centres timing needed to keep according to the feasibility of time of adults.

Another implication is that environment of centre was not congenial thus, needed to be improved by providing library facilities, by increasing honorarium of instructors and supervisors, providing more training to instructors and supervisors and providing more teaching-learning material to the centres.

Appendix A

Retention Test for Adult Learners

भाग–I

1. **लिखिए–**

नाम...

पिता/पति का नाम...

व्यवसाय... लिंग..................................

आय (मासिक)...................................... गाँव..................................

डाकखाना.. तहसील..............................

जिला.. राज्य..................................

प्रौढशिक्षा केन्द्र का नाम...

2. **पहचानिये–**

नीचे कुछ शब्द दिए गए हैं। ( ) में एक शब्द दिया गया है। उसे इन शब्दों से पहचान कर उसके उपर (✓) का निशान लगाएं :

1.	ठ	श	ह	र	म	(ह)
2.	꠸	छ	न	क	थ	(न)
3.	ग	स्र	य	ज	ख	(स)
4.	तू	टू	पे	ऐ	सै	(पे)
5.	ओ	वु	यु	गु	दि	(यु)

3. **नीचे लिखे अक्षरों को जोड़कर शब्द बनाइये :**

1. आ + म =

2. रा + म =
3. र + मा =
4. आ + या =
5. गा + ना =
6. श + ह + र =
7. न + म + क =
8. क + म + ला =
9. र + शी + द =
10. अ + न + थ + क =

4. साल के महीनों के नाम लिखिए।

5. नीचे दिए पहरे को पढ़कर अन्त में दिए गए प्रश्नों के उत्तर दें।

नरातों में बाहू माता का मेला लगा हुआ था। मेले में बड़ी चहल-पहल थी। लोगों ने रंग-बिरंगे कपड़े पहने हुए थे। मिठाई की दुकानें सजी थीं। चूड़ियों की दुकान पर लड़कियों की भीड़ थी। ढोल की आवाज चारों ओर गूंज रही थी। राजू और लता भी सुखना देने सब से पहले बाहू माता के मन्दिर में आए थे।

प्रश्न–

1. नरातों में क्या हुआ ?
2. मिठाई की दुकानें कैसी थी ?
3. चूड़ियों की दुकान पर क्या था ?
4. लोगों ने कैसे कपड़े पहने थे ?
5. राजू और लता बाहू के मन्दिर में क्यों आए थे ?

6. खाली स्थान भरिए–

1. गन्दगी.................लाती है। (गरीबी, कमाई, बीमारी)
2. ....पीना ठीक नहीं। (शराब, पानी, चाय)
3. शाम उनके................देखता रहा। (बाट, कंगन, ठाठ)

भाग-II

1. नीचे लिखी गिनतियाँ पूरी करें–

(1) 1.............. 3.............. 6.............. 8.............. 10..............

(2) 12............. 15............. 18............. 20.............

(3) 30............. 32............. 35............. 37............. 40............

(4) 52............. 55............. 57............. 59............. 61............

(5) 88............. 91............. 94............. 96............. 99............

2. (1) एक सप्ताह में.............दिन होते हैं।

(2) एक साल में.............दिन होते हैं।

(3) एक रुपए में.............नये पैसे होते हैं।

(4) एक किलोग्राम में.............ग्राम होते हैं।

(5) एक क्विंटल में.............किलोग्राम होते हैं।

3. जोडिए–

उदाहरण–
$$\begin{array}{r} 10 \\ +\ 1 \\ \hline 11 \\ \hline \end{array}$$

(1) $\begin{array}{r} 20 \\ +\ 1 \\ \hline \\ \hline \end{array}$ (2) $\begin{array}{r} 30 \\ +\ 8 \\ \hline \\ \hline \end{array}$ (3) $\begin{array}{r} 40 \\ +10 \\ \hline \\ \hline \end{array}$ (4) $\begin{array}{r} 60 \\ +10 \\ \hline \\ \hline \end{array}$ (5) $\begin{array}{r} 88 \\ +112 \\ \hline \\ \hline \end{array}$

4. घटाइए–

उदाहरण–
$$\begin{array}{r} 10 \\ -\ 1 \\ \hline 09 \\ \hline \end{array}$$

(1)	(2)	(3)	(4)	(5)
2 0	3 2	7 9	9 0	135
- 1	- 9	- 1 9	- 1	- 101
____	____	____	____	____

5. कुल कितने रुपये-पैसे हुए ?

रुपये	पैसे
12	35
9	65
7	90

6. शामू ने अपने बेटे राम को 10 रुपये और मोहन को 15 रुपये दिए। बताइए शामू ने अपने बेटों को कुल कितने रुपये दिए ?

7. हमीद के पास 35 भैसें थी। उसने 22 भैंसें बेच दीं। बताइए उसके पास कितनी भैसें रह गई ?

8. राम के पास एक 20 रुपये का नोट, एक 10 रुपये का नोट, एक 2 रुपये का नोट, एक 1 रुपये का नोट है। बताइए राम के पास कुल कितने रुपये हैं।

9. एक सन्तरे की कीमत 25 पैसे है। 4 सन्तरों की कितनी कीमत होगी ?

10. एक अन्डे की कीमत 70 पैसे है। 5 सन्तरों की कितनी कीमत होगी ?

11. श्याम के पास 20 सेब हैं और दस लड़कों को उसने पूरे-पूरे बाँटने हैं। बताइए एक लड़के को कितने सेब मिलेगें ?

12. रीता के घर की आमदनी 500 रुपये है। उसने कपड़े खरीदने पर 30 रुपये खाने-पीने की वस्तुएं खरीदने पर 200 रुपये बीज और खाद खरीदने पर 35 रुपये खर्च किए। बताइए उसके पास कितने रुपये बाकी रह गए ?

भाग-III

1. **खाली स्थानों को भरिये–**

    1. प्रधानमंत्री का नाम...
    2. मुख्य मंत्री का नाम...
    3. ग्राम प्रधान का नाम..
    4. प्रौढ़ शिक्षक/शिक्षिका का नाम...
    5. देश का नाम...

2. **नीचे लिखे हुए वाक्यों को पढ़कर हाँ अथवा नहीं पर (✓) का निशान लगाएं–**

1.	लड़की की शादी 18 वर्ष से कम आयु में होनी चाहिए।	हाँ/नहीं
2.	बच्चों को अच्छा पढ़ाना लिखाना चाहिए।	हाँ/नहीं
3.	औरतें समाज का जरूरी अंग हैं।	हाँ/नहीं
4.	शादी में दहेज लेना व देना घोर अपराध है।	हाँ/नहीं
5.	पढ़ने लिखने से जानकारी बढ़ती है।	हाँ/नहीं
6.	औंरतों को सरकारी नौकरी करनी चाहिए।	हाँ/नही
7.	हमें अपने घर की सफाई रखनी चाहिए।	हाँ/नहीं
8.	हमें अपने गांव की सफाई रखनी चाहिए।	हाँ/नही
9.	परिवार में ज्यादा बच्चे होना ठीक नहीं।	हाँ/नहीं
10.	गर्भवती महिलाओं का खास ध्यान रखना चाहिए।	हाँ/नही
11.	शराब पीना सेहत के लिए हानिकारक है।	हाँ/नही
12.	एकता में बल है।	हाँ/नहीं
13.	हमारी सरकार लोकतंत्रीय है।	हाँ/नहीं
14.	चुनाव में वोट देने जाना हमारा कर्तव्य है।	हाँ/नहीं
15.	हमारे देश की सत्ताधारी पार्टी का नाम भाजपा है।	हाँ/नहीं
16.	अपनी कमाई से हमें कुछ बचाना चाहिए।	हाँ/नहीं
17.	बचाए हुए पैसे को जमा करवाना चाहिए।	हाँ/नहीं

18. बैंक में जमा राशि से हमें लाभ होता है। हाँ/नहीं
19. बैंक में हमें आसान किस्तों पर कर्जा मिल सकता है। हाँ/नहीं
20. बच्चों को पौष्टिक आहार देना चाहिए। हाँ/नहीं
21. बच्चों को डाक्टर की सलाह पर टीके लगवाने चाहिए। हाँ/नहीं
22. घर में हमें प्यार से रहना चाहिए। हाँ/नहीं
23. हमें गांव में मिल-जुल कर रहना चाहिए। हाँ/नहीं
24. गांव में सरकारी समितियां बनानी चाहिए। हाँ/नहीं
25. धार्मिक ग्रन्थ पढ़ने चाहिएं। हाँ/नहीं
26. हमें दूसरे धर्म के मानने वालों से नफरत नहीं करनी चाहिए। हाँ/नहीं
27. हमें कर्तव्य का पालन करना चाहिए। हाँ/नहीं
28. हमें बडों की आज्ञा का पालन करना चाहिए। हाँ/नहीं
29. राष्ट्रीय त्योहारों को धूम-धाम से मनाना चाहिए। हाँ/नहीं
30. अपने हक के लिए हमें लड़ना चाहिए। हाँ/नहीं
31. समाज की कुरीतियां दूर करना हमारा कर्तव्य है। हाँ/नहीं
32. अस्पृश्यता एक सामाजिक बुराई है। हाँ/नहीं
33. हमें गरीबों की सहायता करनी चाहिए। हाँ/नहीं
34. खेतीबाड़ी वैज्ञानिक ढंग से करनी चाहिए। हाँ/नहीं
35. रासायनिक खाद डालने से भूमि बंजर हो जाती है। हाँ/नहीं
36. फसलों के बीज सरकार द्वारा प्रमाणित ही लगाने चाहिए। हाँ/नहीं
37. डाकखाने द्वारा हम पत्र एक स्थान से दूसरे स्थान पर भेज सकते हैं। हाँ/नहीं
38. हम मनीआर्डर द्वारा पैसे भेज सकते हैं। हाँ/नहीं
39. हमें बड़ों का आदर करना चाहिए। हाँ/नहीं
40. हमें सड़क के दांए ओर चलना चाहिए। हाँ/नहीं
41. बच्चों के चरित्र निर्माण में परिवार का योगदान आवश्यक है। हाँ/नहीं
42. हमें वनों की रक्षा करनी चाहिए। हाँ/नहीं

Appendix B

Interview Schedule for Adult Learners

1. Name...
2. Name of the Centre/Village...
3. Sex: Male/Female...
4. Age (in years)..
5. Occupations..
6. Caste (specify if SC/ST)..
7. Religion...
8. Annual family income...
9. Literate members of the family...
10. Location of your house (whether on the outskirts of the village or farther away from the centre)

    ....
11. Is this programme suited to your interests? Yes/No
12. (a) Did you join the centre willingly to learn? Yes/No

    (b) If yes, what reasons made you to join the centre?

    ....

    (c) If not, who persuaded you to join the class?

    ....
13. What type of reading material do you get from the centre?

    ....
14. (a) Do you have library facilities? Yes/No

    (b) If yes, what kind of books do you get out of the libraries?

    ....

15. What is the duration of the programme?

    ....

16. Do you think duration is sufficient for completion of the course? Yes/No

17. How much time did you take to learn?

    ....

18. Are you able to write independently? Yes/No

19. Did you like learning in a group? Yes/No

20. Can you write a letter to your own? Yes/No

21. Does the teaching methods suit to your interests?Yes/No

22. Does your teacher teach you by narrating stories?Yes/No

23. Does your teacher teach you by Laubach Method?Yes/No

    (Teaching from simple charts representing a phrase, a word and the first letter of the word combined with pictures)

24. Does your teacher teach you by Analytical Method?

    Yes/No

    (Starts from sentences and then proceeds to words and so on)

25. (a) Is there post-literacy practice for ex-learners?

    Yes/No

    (b) If yes, what is the duration of the class?

    ....

    ....

26. What reasons do you think for dropouts?

    ....

    ....

27. Do you think this programme will help you to raise your standard of living? Yes/No

28. Was your presence in Adult Education Centre at the cost of your time to be devoted in farm/agriculture? Yes/No

29. Will study through Adult Education Programme help you to introduce innovations for improving production of your work? Yes/No
30. Do you think something more should be taught for improvement in the production of your work? Yes/No

Appendix C

Interview Schedule for Instructors

1. Name of the Centre/Village..
2. Instructor's Name..
3. Address..
4. Sex: Male/Female..
5. Age (in years)..
6. Caste: SC/ST/Others..
7. Occupations (with details of nature of work)

   ....
8. Educational qualification..
9. (a) Are you from the same village? Yes/No

   (b) If not, what is the distance from your place of living to the centre?

   ....
10. Mention your involvement in the past in any socially constructive, developmental, community activities.

    ....
11. Reasons for becoming an instructor in AEC.

    ....
12. How were you selected?

    (Give details about the persons who contacted you and the manner you got in touch with the agency etc.)

    ....

    ....
13. (a) Were you trained for teaching in AEC? Yes/No

    (b) If yes, give details:

(*i*) Name of the training centre....................................

(*ii*) Duration of training..

(*iii*) Content...

(*iv*) Methodology...

14. What aspects of your training are helpful in running the AEC?

....

15. What are your suggestions to improve training programme for instructors?

....

16. How did you recruit the learners?

(Give details e.g. through conducting surveys, taking help of others, etc.)

....

17. What problems did you face in identifying the learners?

....

18. What are your suggestions for future in identifying and enrolling the learners?

....

19. What is content of teaching?

(Give details regarding literacy, functionality and social awareness)

....

20. What methods are you using to teach the components of Adult Education?

....

21. What are the various kinds of learning experiences you are providing to the learners?

....

22. What are the other activities that you are providing to the learners?

....

23. What do you think about the programme in general?

....

24. What are the various difficulties you are facing in running the centres? (Prove in relation to agency, supervisor, supply of material, finances, location, learners, attitude of villagers etc.)

....

25. What are your specific suggestions to run these centres?

....

26. What kind of support do you expect from the supervisor and the agency? (Other than facilities and equipments)

....

27. What reasons do you think for dropouts?

....

28. What are your suggestions to bring dropouts back to the centres?

....

29. What are your experience of running this centre in relation to literacy, functionality and social awareness?

    (Prove your altitude, difficulties and achievement in relation to literacy, functionality and social awareness).

30. Are you getting sufficient support from the agency which established the AECs ? (In the form of literature, visual pictures and other equipments). Yes/No

Appendix D

Supervisory Level, Interview Schedule

1. Name..
2. Age (in years)...
3. Sex (Male/Female)...
4. Educational qualifications..
5. Caste..
6. Previous Experience...
7. Since how long are you in this agency?

   ....
8. What the activities in which you are actively involved?

   ....
9. What strategy are you using in relation to:
   (a) Identification of villages,
   (b) Location of AECs,
   (c) Identification of instructors,
   (d) Training of instructors, and
   (e) Monitoring the activities of AECs (To be recorded in details)

   ....

   ....
10. What are your experiences in relation to the above (a, b, c, d, e)?

    ....

11. How did you choose this assignment?

    ....

12. List the various difficulties and problems faced by you in relation to:

    (a) Identification of village/towns/cities.

    (b) Identification of instructors.

    (c) Identification of teaching materials.

    ....

    ....

    ....

    (d) Training...

    (e) Collaboration from other agencies

    ....

    (f) Supply of materials

    ....

    (g) Motivation of learners etc.

    ....

13. What do you know about the programme as it is running?

    ....

    ....

14. What are your suggestions and views in improving the programme?

    ....

    ....

15. How do you evaluate the performance of instructors?

    ....

    ....

16. What kind of tools do you adopt for evaluating the performance of instructors?

....

....

17. What kind of parameters do you evaluate?

....

18. (a) Is there any procedure for bringing improvements after evaluation? Yes/No

    (b) If yes, please specify..

19. What is the frequency of the visits of supervisors to Adult Education Centres for evaluation?

....

....

Appendix E

Interview Schedule for Agency: University/College

1. Name of the University/College..
2. When did you launch your programme?..............................

   ....
3. Were all the centres started simultaneously? Yes/No
4. What is the number of centres run by the University/College?

   Give the details:

Location of the Centre	*For Male*	*For Female*	*Mixed*	*For SC*	*For other backward classes*	*Total*

5. What are the reasons for starting the centres?
   (a) Geographical affinity ( )
   (b) Backwardness of the village/region/people ( )
   (c) Local initiative of the people ( )

(d) Political point of view ( )

(e) Others (please specify) ( )

6. Number of centres recommended by the University/ College to the UGC/Govt. year-wise.

....

....

7. Number of centres sanctioned by UGC/Govt. year-wise.

....

8. Please give the details of training:

(*i*) For Instructors:

(a) Name of training institution..

(b) Duration of training..

(c) Daily training hours..

(d) Place of training..

(e) Teaching methods used...

(*ii*) For Supervisors:

(a) Name of training institution..

(b) Duration of training..

(c) Daily training hours..

(d) Place of training..

(e) Teaching methods used...

9. Please indicate broadly methods of selecting instructors and supervisors.

(a) Supervisory practice and monitoring.

(b) Basis of selection of village/centre.

....

....

10. Please list the materials that you have been able to provide to all the centres.

....

11. Mention the nature of follow-up activities that you conduct in closed centres.

....

....

12. Is the programme continuously going on year-wise? Yes/No

13. What changes have you introduced in respect of number of centres and location of centres?

....

....

14. Have you introduced changes in respect of target groups? Yes/No

(Please specify Male/Female	*Mixed*	*Backward Classes*	*SC/ST)*

15. Have you introduced any change in method of selection of instructors and supervisors? Yes/No
(If yes, please specify)

....

....

16. How much time was involved in submitting the proposal and receiving the government sanction?

....

17. Is the Government/UGC grant received in time? Yes/No

18. Is the grant adequate to meet your needs? Yes/No

19. What is your opinion regarding the success of running the centres?

Satisfactory/Casual/Unsatisfactory

20. Please indicate the major difficulties you have faced in running the AECs.

    (Administrative/Financial/Operational)

    ....

21. Would you like to make any specific suggestion to improve the adult education programme? Yes/No

    (If yes, please specify)

22. Mention some of the significant learning experiences since the time you have started the programme?

    ....

    ....

Bibliography

Aggarwal, J.C. (1971), "*UNESCO Contribution Towards World Education*", Arya Book Depot, New Delhi.

Aggarwal, J.C. (1975), "*Educational Research—An Introduction*". Arya Book Depot, New Delhi.

Aggarwal, Y.P. (1988), "*Research in Emerging Fields of Education, Concepts, Trends and Prospects*", Sterling Publishers Private Limited, New Delhi.

Agnihotri, S. (1974), "*Evaluation of the Programme of Adult Education in Operation under Pilot Plan in Wardha District*", Ph.D. Education, Nagpur University.

Ahmed, M. & Srivastava, N.K. (1995), "*A Comparative Study of the Analytic and Synthetic Methods of Teaching*", National Literacy Mission, New Delhi.

Ahmed, M. and Coombs, H.P. (1975), "*Education for Rural Development: Case Studies for Planners*", Praeger Publishers, New York.

Altbach, G.P. *et al.* (1982), "*Comparative Education*", McMillan Publishing Company Inc, New York.

Ambasht, N.K. (1970), "*A Critical Study of Tribal Education (With Special Reference to Ranchi District)*", S. Chand & Co., New Delhi.

Ansari, N.A. (1984), "*Adult Education in India*", S. Chand and Company Limited, New Delhi.

Bandari, J.S. (1974), "*Factors Affecting Persistency and Dropout of Adult Literacy Classes in Udaipur District*", Ph.D. Agriculture, Udaipur University.

Bastia, K.C. (1982), "*A Study of National Adult Education Programme in the Tribal Region of Orissa*", Ph.D. Education, M.S. University.

Best, W.B. and Kahn, James (1995), "*Research in Education* (*Seventh Edition*), Prentice Hall in India Private Limited, New Delhi.

Bhageria, R. (1992), *"The Impact of Polyvalent Education of Shramik Vidyapeeths on Industrial Workers"*, Ph.D. Education, Punjabi University.

Bhat, S.S. (1992), *"Growth and Development of Adult Education"*, Cosomo Publishing, New Delhi.

Bhatia, S.C. and Patel, B.R. (1983), *"Research in Adult Education"*, Indian Adult Education Association, New Delhi.

Bordia, A. (1973), *"Adult Education in India"*, A Book of Readings, Nachiketa Publications Limited, Bombay.

Bordia, A. (1975), *"Farmers Training and Functional Literacy"*, Indian Adult Education Association, New Delhi.

Buch, M.B. (1979), *"Survey of Research in Education, 1972-78"*, Society for Educational Research and Development, Baroda.

Chaturvedi, S.C. (1969), *"Impact of Social Education on the Life and Living of the People in Block Areas (In districts of Gorakhpur, Jhansi, Lucknow and Mathura)"*, Ph.D., Social Work, Lucknow University.

Chopra, R. (1989), *"Developing Learning Package for Illiterate Adults and Testing their Effectiveness: An Experimental Study"*, Ph.D. Edu., Kurukshetra University.

Chopra, Rita (1993), *"Adult Education in India"*, Himalaya Publishing House, Delhi.

Choudhary, K.C. & Sachdeva, J.L. (1995), *"Total Literacy by 2000"*, Indian Adult Education Association, New Delhi.

Cochran, G.W. (1974), *"Sampling Techniques"*, Wiley Eastern Private Limited, New Delhi.

Coles, E. K. Townsend (1977), *"Adult Education in Developing Countries"*, Pergamon Press Oxford.

Coombs, H.P. (1985), *"The World Crisis in Education"*, The View From Eighties, Oxford University Press.

David, B.R. (1972), *"Priorities in Adult Education"*, MacMillan, New York.

Deisey, J. (1916), *"Democracy and Education"*, McMillan Company, New York.

Deswani, C.J. (1985), *"Role of Universities in Rural Literacy Campaign"*, Indian Journal of Adult Education, Vol. 46, No.1.

Dey, B.R. and Tarajon, R. (1981), *"Evaluation of Adult Education Programme in Nine Districts in Bihar"*, Xavier Institute, Jamshedpur.

Directorate of Adult Education (1990), *"Literacy Digest: Based on 1991 Census"*, New Delhi.

Directorate of Adult Education (1987), *"Crusade against Illiteracy"*, New Delhi.

Directorate of Adult Education (1990), *"Campaign for Literacy: Some Thoughts on Adult Education"*, New Delhi.

Directorate of Adult Education (1989), *"Literacy for All: Some Thoughts on Adult Education"*, New Delhi.

Dixit, A.A. (1972), *"A Study of Educational Need Pattern of Adults in Urban, Rural and Tribal Communities of Rajasthan"*, Ph.D. Education, Rajasthan University.

Doreu, M.V. (1959), *"Liberal Education"*, Beacon Press, Boston.

Dutta, S.C. (1959), *"On to Eternity"*, Indian Adult Education Association, New Delhi.

Dutta, S.C. (1960), *"Social Education in Delhi"*, Indian Adult Education Association, New Delhi.

Dutta, S.C. (1966), *"New Trends in Adult Education in India"*, Indian Adult Education Association, New Delhi.

Dutta, S.C. (1986), *"Adult Education in India"*, Indian Adult Education Association, New Delhi.

Dutta, S.C. and Fisher, H.J. (1972), *"Training of Adult Educators"*, Shakuntla Publishing House, Bombay.

Ellywood, C. (1976), *"Adult Learning Today"*, A New Role for the University London, Sage Publications.

Essent. L.P. (1951), *"Creative Leadership of Adult Education"*, Prentice Hall Inc., New York.

Faure, E. (1972), *"Learning To Be"*, UNESCO, Paris.

Furst, E.J. (1961), *"Constructing Evaluation Instruments"*, Longmans, New York.

Garrett, H.E. and Woodworth, R.S. (1981), *"Statistics in Psychology and Education"*, Vakils, Feffers and Simons Limited, Bombay.

Gayatonde, N.V. (1977), *"The Problem of Social Education in India with Special Reference to Maharashtra, Gujarat, Rajasthan, Madhya Pradesh, Mysore (Karnataka),"* Ph.D., Education, Poona University.

Gode, M.A. (1979), "*Handbook for Functionaries of NAEP in University and Colleges*", Bombay.

Good, C.V. (1973), "*Dictionary of Education*", McGraw Hill, New York.

Government of India, "*Challenge of Education—A Policy Perspective*", Ministry of Education and Culture, New Delhi, 1985.

Hemlatha, C. (1987), "*Receptivity to Adult Education Programme and Factors Influencing the Process*", Ph.D., Osmania University.

Howe, J.A. (1977), "*Adult Learning: Psychology Research and Application*", John Wiley and Sons, London.

Hwang, J.G. (1982), "*Adult Education and Industrial Urban Development*, UNESCO", Adult Education in Asia and Pacific, Special Issue, UNESCO, Bangkok.

Indian Adult Education Association, "*1991-2001—A Decade Literacy: Role of State and Civil Society*", Indian Journal of Adult Education, Vol. 63, No. 2, 2002.

Indian Adult Education Association, "*Retention of Literacy by Adult Learners in Nellore District Andhra Pradesh*", Indian Journal of Adult Education, Vol. 64, No. 2, 2003.

Indian Adult Education Association, Indian Journal of Adult Education, Vol. 49 No. 3, July-September 1988, New Delhi.

Indian Adult Education Association, Indian Journal of Adult Education, Vol. 50 No. 1, January to March 1989, New Delhi.

Indian Adult Education Association, Indian Journal of Adult Education, Vol. 50 No.2, April- June 1989, New Delhi.

Indian University Association for Continuing Education and Extension: Programme in Universities and Colleges, 1988, New Delhi.

Jain, S.P., Bawa, P.S. and Gupta, S.C. (1984). "*Research in Adult Education in India: A Select Bibliography*", Directorate of Adult Education, New Delhi.

Janardhan Reddy, G. (1988), "*Persuasion of Adult Learners: A Study*", Indian Journal of Adult Education Vol. 49, No. 3, July-September 1988, New Delhi.

Jarvis, P. (1987), "*Twentieth Century Thinkers in Adult Education*", Published by Groom Helin in Association with Methuen Inc., New York.

Jarvis, P. (1987), *"Adult Learning in Social Context"*, Croom Helin, London.

Jayagopal, R. (1985), *"Adult Learning, Department of Adult and Continuing Education"*, University of Madras.

Jenkis, J. (1981), *"Material for Learning: How to Teach Adult at a Distance"*, Routeledge and Kegan Paul, London.

Johnson J.P. (1970), *"A Proposal for the Establishment of a State-wide Adult Education Programme for Madras (Tamil Nadu)"*, Ph.D, Education, Madras University.

Jolly, K.G. (1992), *"Literacy for All by 2000"*, B.R. Publishing Corporation, New Delhi.

Kaul P.N. (1970), *"Attitude Towards Extension Education of Under Graduate Agricultural University Teachers at Various Stages in Their Instructions"*, Ph.D., Agriculture Extension Education, P.A.U.

Kaur, K. (1988), *"Learning Choices of Illiterate Adults in Border District of Punjab"*, Indian Journal of Adult Education, Vol. 49, No. 3, July to September, IAEA, New Delhi.

Kaur, Pushpinder (1998), *"Factors Which Motivate Rural Female Adults to Participate in the Adult Education Programme in Relation to Some Selected Socio-Personal and Economic Factors"*, Ph.D. Education, Punjabi University.

Kemfer, H. (1955), *"Adult Education"*, McGraw Hill Book Company Inc., New York.

Kerlinger, F.N. (1973), *"Foundation of Behavioural Research"*, Holt, Rinehart and Winston, Inc., New York.

Khajapeer, M. (1978), *"A Study of the Academic Performance of Farmers' Functional Literacy Programme Participants in Relation to Some Socio-Psychological Factors"*, Ph.D. Education, S.V.U.

Khandai, H.K. (1995), *"Preparation of a Manual for Developing Literature for Neo-Literates"*, Ph.D. Education, Devi Ahilya Vishawa-Vidyalaya.

Kiwia, F.N.S. (1989), *"Functional Literacy and Development in Tanzania: Perspectives in Education"*, A Journal of SERD, Vol. 5, No. 1, Baroda.

Knox, B.A. (1977), *"Adult Development and Learning"*, Jossey Bass, Inc. Publisher, California.

Kudesia, U.C. (1973), *"The Role of Social Education in Rural Development of Madhya Pradesh"*, Ph.D. Education, Sagar University.

Kundu, C.L. (1985), *"Jurisprudential Method for Developing Social Awareness Among Adults"*, Indian Journal of Adult Education, Vol. 46, No. 6-7, New Delhi.

Kundu, C.L. (1985), *"Adult Education Numeracy Modules"*, Centre for Adult Education and Extension, Kurukshetra.

Kundu, C.L. (1986), *"Adult Education, Principles, Practice and Prospectus"*, Sterling Publishers Private Limited, New Delhi.

Kundu, C.L. (1987), *"Adult Education Research: Future Directions"*, Kurukshetra University.

Kundu, C.L. (1994), *"Adult Education Programme in the University System"*, Nirmal Book, Kurukshetra.

Lalthankingi (1998), *"An Appraisal of Adult Education in Mizoram"*, Ph.D. Education, NEHU.

Lund, R. (1952), *"Scandinavian Adult Education"*, Publishers Dept. Danske Forlag, Copenhegan.

Mahanty, S.C. (1991), *"National Adult Education Programme in India"*, Chugh Publications, Allahabad.

Malgarkar, D.P. (1988), *"A Micro Analysis of Adult Education in India"*, National Book Organization, New Delhi.

Mali, M.G. (1974), *"Factors Affecting Retention of Literacy Among Adult Neo-Literates"*, Ph.D. Education, Shi University.

Mali, M.G. (1984), *"Adult Education in India"*, Deep and Deep Publications, New Delhi.

Mansari, R.D. (1959), *"Second All India Adult Conference on to Eternity"*, Indian Adult Education Association, New Delhi.

Mascarenhas, M.M. (1982), *"Population Education for Quality of Life"*, Oxford and IBH Publishing Company, New Delhi.

Mathur, B. and Rajindra, M. (1989), *"Adult Education and Social Change"*, Indian Publication, Ambala.

Miller, H.L. (1964), *"Teaching and Learning in Adult Education"*, MacMillan, New York.

Ministry of Education and Culture, Report of the Review Committee on the National Adult Education Programme, Government of India, New Delhi, 1980.

Ministry of Education and Social Welfare, *"National Adult Education Programme"*, An Outline, Government of India, New Delhi, 1979.

Ministry of Education, Report of the Education Commission 1964-66, Government of India, 1978.

Ministry of Human Resource Development, Department of Education, National Literacy Mission (Draft), New Delhi, 1987.

Ministry of Human Resource Development, Jan Shikshan Nilayam, New Delhi, 1988.

Ministry of Human Resource Development, National Policy on Education, New Delhi, 1986.

Mohanthy, S.B. (1988), "*Life Long and Adult Education*", Ashish Publishing House, New Delhi.

Mohanthy, S.B. (1985), "*Non-Formal Education*", Chugh Publications, Allahabad.

Mohanty, B.B. & Sachdeva, J.L. (1992), "*Approaches to Total Literacy*", Indian Adult Education Association, New Delhi.

Mohanty, B.B. (1989), "*Adult Education: Some Reflections*", Indian Adult Education Association, New Delhi.

Mohanty, J. (2002), "*Adult and Non-Formal Education*", Deep and Deep, New Delhi.

Mohsini, H.R. (1992), "*History of Adult Education in India*", Anmol Publishing, New Delhi.

Monreo (1856), "*Encyclopedia of Educational Research*", Macmillan Company, New York.

Mydum R. (1993), "*An Evaluation of National Adult Education Programme in Warangal District*", Ph.D. Education, Kakatiya University.

Myrdal G. Asian Drama, "*An Enquiry into the Poverty of Nations*", Pantheon, New York.

Najmi, N.N. (1971), "*Social Education in Haryana, Education in Haryana: Retrospect and Prospect*", by Uday Shankar and C.L. Kundu, Kurukshetra University.

Natarajan, P. (1995), "*Impact of Literacy Efforts in Tamil Nadu*", Ph.D. Education, Annamalai University.

National Institute of Adult Education (2000), "*Education for All*", New Delhi.

National Literacy Mission (1992), "*Literacy: A People's Movement*", New Delhi.

National Literacy Mission (1997), "*Literacy Facts at a Glance*", Directorate of Adult Education, New Delhi.

National Literacy Mission (1997), *"Towards A Literate India"*, Directorate of Adult Education, New Delhi.

National Literacy Mission (2000), *"Education for All"*, National Institute of Adult Education, New Delhi.

National Policy on Education—1986, *"Cited in Education Policy and Implementation"*, Special Issue, Indian Journal of Public Administration, Quarterly, Vol. XXXII, No. 3, New Delhi.

Newman, Michael, Poor Cousin (1979), *"A Study of Adult Education"*, George Allen and Unwin, Boston.

Nimbalkay, M.R. (1987), *"Adult Education and Its Evaluation System"*, Mittal Publications, New Delhi.

Panda, S.K. and Sarangi, H. (1988), *"Universities and Adult Education Research"*, Indian Journal of Adult Education, Vol. 3, July-September.

Pankajam, G. (1988), *"Role and Functions of College Teachers and Students in Adult and Continuing Education Programmes"*, Indian Journal of Adult Education, Vol. 49, No. 3, July-September.

Patel, Moghanand (1995), *"Jan Shikshan Nilayam Programme in Tribal Areas of Orissa: An Evaluative Study"*, Ph.D. Education, Himachal Pradesh University.

Patel, T. (1984), *"Development of Education Among Tribal Women"*, Mittal Publishers, New Delhi.

Pati, S.P. (1997), *"Problems of Adult Education Programmes"*, The Indian Publication, Ambala.

Pati, Sura Prasad (1989), *"Adult Education"*, Ashish Publishing House, New Delhi.

Pestonjee, D.M. (1981), *"National Adult Education Programme in Rajasthan"*, Second Appraisal, IIM, Ahmedabad.

Pillai, K.S. (1975), *"Education in a New Perspective: A Plea for Continuous, Non-Formal Functional Education and Certain Research Findings on Functional Literacy Programme in Kerala"*, College Book House, Trivandrum.

Prakash, V. (1987), *"Student Aspirations: Some Misconceptions"*, Mittal Publications, Delhi.

Prasad, D.R. (1991), *"Adult Education"*, Ashish Publishing House, New Delhi.

Rahi, A.H. (1996), "*Adult Education Policies and Programmes*", The Associate Press, Ambala Cantt.

Ramabrahman, I. (1988), "*Adult Education Policy and Performance*", Gian Publishing House, New Delhi.

Rao, T.V. (1980), "*Adult Education for Social Change*", Manohar Publications, New Delhi.

Rao, V.K.R.V. (1970), "*Adult Education and National Development*", Ministry of Education and Youth Services, New Delhi.

Reddy, Narayana (1997), "*A Critical Study of Development of Adult Education in Andhra Pradesh during the Post-Independent Period*", Ph.D. Education, Osmania University.

Reddy, P.A. (1970), "*Adult Education Programme in India*", Chugh Publications, Allahabad.

Rehman, S. (1982), "*Communication Technology for Adult Education*", Reading in Educational Technology by B. Anand Rao and S. Ravishankar, Himilaya Publishing House, Bombay.

Rouch, D.B. (1972), "*Priorities in Adult Education*", MacMillan, New York.

Roy, N.R. (1967), "*Adult Education in India and Abroad*", S. Chand and Company, New Delhi.

Roy, P. & Kapoor, J.M. (1975), "*The Retention of Literacy*", MacMillan Company of India Ltd., Delhi.

Russel, B. (1980), "*Education and Social Order*", Unwin Paperbacks, London.

Sachdeva, J.L. (1989), "*Adult Education Terminology*", Indian Adult Education Association, New Delhi.

Salamatullah and Deo Bareth, (1984), "*Adult Education Research in India: A Study*", Indian Adult Education Association.

Sambaiah, (1982), "*Organisation and Working of NAEP in Andhra Pradesh*", M.Phil., Department of Public Administration, Kakatiya University.

Seethuramu, A.S. (1994), "*Adult Education*", APH Publishing Corporation, New Delhi.

Seth, M. (1982), "*Motivation in Adult Learners Participating in Functional Literacy Programme in Delhi*", Ph.D. H.Sc., Delhi University.

Seth, M. (1986), "*Mass Education Involving College Students in Instruction: A Case Study*", Indian Journal of Adult Education.

Shah, A. and Siva Laxami, K. (1988), "*Each One Teach Another· Baroda Experiment*", Indian Journal of Adult Education, Vol. 49, No. 3, July-September.

Shah, A.B. and Bhan, S. (1980), "*Non-Formal Education and the NAEP*", Oxford University Press, New Delhi.

Shah, A.J. (1979), "*A Critical Study of the Programmes of the Non-Formal Education in Baroda City and Their Impact on the Community*", Ph.D. Education, M.S. University.

Shah, S.Y. (1989), "*Adult Education in Bihar*", Indian Adult Education Association, New Delhi.

Shah, S.Y. (1991), "*Each one Teach One—Laubach's Materials and Methods*", Indian Adult Education Association, New Delhi.

Sharma, A. (1989), "*Adult Education in India*", Anmol Publications, New Delhi.

Sharma, A. *et al.* (1979), "*Adult Education in Gujarat: An Appraisal*", Sardar Patel Institute of Economic and Social Research, Ahmedabad.

Sharma, D.V. (1984), "*In Search of a Conceptual Framework of Adult Education, Reading Material*", VI, Directorate of Adult Education, Bangalore.

Sharma, *et al.* (1981), "*Adult Education Programme in Gujarat—Revisited*", Sardar Patel Institute of Economic and Social Research, Ahmedabad.

Sharma, I.P. (1985), "*Adult Education in India: A Policy Perspective*", NBO Publishers, Distribution, New Delhi.

Sharma, I.P. (1986), "*Adult Education in India, A Programme of Action: Education Policy and Implementation*", The Indian Journal of Public Administration, Vol. XXXII, No. 3, July-September.

Sharma, R.A. (1984), "*Fundamental of Educational Research*", Loyal Book Depot, Meerut.

Singh Dhanipal (1997), "*A Study of Voluntary Organisations in Rajasthan and the Impact of their Educational Programmes*", Ph.D. Education, Vidyabhawan Higher Educational Institute, Udaipur.

Singh, A.K. (1988), "*A Micro Analysis of Adult Education in India*", National Book Organisation, New Delhi.

Singh, Madan (1994), *"Impact of Adult Education Programme in Modernisation of Learners in Sarojini Nagar Block of Lucknow District"*, Ph.D. Education, Lucknow University.

Singh, Priti (1988), *"An Investigation into Aptitudes of Adult Education Functionaries Towards National Adult Education Programme in Relation to Their Personality Traits"*, Ph.D. Education, Kurukshetra University.

Singh, R. (1989), *"Development Awareness Among Illiterate Adults—An Experiment"*, Indian Journal of Adult Education, Vol. 1, January-March, New Delhi.

Singh, R.P. (1987), *"Non-Formal Education, An Alternative Approach"*, Sterling Publishers Private Limited, New Delhi.

Singh, Rajinder (1988), *"Adult Education Training and Productivity"*, Ph.D. Education, Kurukshetra University.

Singh, Rajindra (1991), *"Adult Education Training and Productivity"* Indian Publication, Ambala Cantt.

Singh, Sohan (1957), *"History of Adult Education in India During British Period"*, Indian Adult Education Association, New Delhi.

Singh, Sohan (1964), *"Social Education in India"*, Government of India, Ministry of Education, New Delhi.

Singh, V.D. (1980), *"The Software for the NAEP"*, Indian Journal of Adult Education, Vol. 41, No. 1-2, New Delhi.

Sinha, P.R. and Kolte, N.V. (1974), *"Adult Education in Relation to Agricultural Development, An Evaluative Study of a Development Block in Andhra Pradesh"*, NICD Hyderabad, India and UNESCO Press, Paris.

Sodhi, H.K. (1993), *"Impact of Adult Education Programme on Attitude of Rural Women Towards Small Family Norms in Relation to Ages, Religion, Family Type and Socio-Economic Status"*, Ph.D. Education, Punjabi University.

Sodhi, T.S. (1985), *"Education and Economic Development"*, Vikas Publishing House, New Delhi.

Sodhi, T.S. and Multani, (1989), *"Comparative Studies in Adult Education"*, The Association Publishers, Ambala.

Styler, W.E. (1966), *"Adult Education in India"*, Oxford University Press, Bombay.

Sultan, P. (1984), "*Adult Education in India: Literacy Language and Social Change*", National Institute of Adult and Continuing Education, Leicester.

Talukdar, B.K.(1975), "*Adult Education in Assam During Post-Independence Period*", Ph.D. Education, Guwahati University.

Tantary, G.N. (1990), "*Adult Education for Jammu & Kashmir: An Appraisal*", Ph.D. Education, University of Jammu.

Thakur, D. (1990), "*Adult Education and Mass Literacy*", Deep and Deep Publications, New Delhi.

Tiwari, B.N. (1980), "*Adult Education and Libraries*", Vohra Publishers and Distributors, Allahabad.

Ubaidullah, M. (1988), "*Population Education: Knowledge and Attitudes of NAEP Participants*", Indian Educational Review, A Research Journal, Vol. XXIII, No. 1.

UNESCO, (1976), "*Draft Recommendation on the Development of Adult Education*", UNESCO, Paris.

UNESCO, (1982), "*Adult Education in Asia and the Pacific Bulletin of the UNESCO*", Regional Office for Education in Asia and the Pacific, Bangkok.

University Grants Commission (1988), "*New Guidelines on Adult and Continuing Education and Extension Programmes in Universities and Colleges*", University Grants Commission, New Delhi.

University Grants Commission, Report for the Year 1973-1974, University Grants Commission, New Delhi.

University Grants Commission, Report for the Year 1977-1978, University Grants Commission, New Delhi.

Vanaja, V. (1989), "*A Study of Women Drop-outs in Adult Education Centres of Mysore Taluk*", Indian Journal of Adult Education, Vol. 1, January-March, New Delhi.

Venkataiah, N. (1977), "*Impact of Farmer's Functional Literacy Programme on the Participants in the Andhra Pradesh*", Ph.D. Education, S.V. University.

Verma, K.K. *et al.* (1981), "*Adult Education for Development: A Study of the National Adult Education Programme in Bihar*", A.N. Sinha Institute of Social Studies, Patna.

Index